# MARGARET BRANDMAN

# HARMONY COMES TOGETHER
## Book One

Four-Part and Three-Part Harmony
Traditional and Modern

Exclusive distributors for Australia and New Zealand
**Encore Music Distributors**
227 Napier St, Fitzroy VIC 3065 Australia
Phone +61 3 9415 6677 Facsimile +61 3 9415 6655
Email: sales@encoremusic.com.au

This book © Copyright 2018 by Margaret Brandman trading as Jazzem Music
46 Gerrale St, Cronulla NSW 2230 Australia
ISBN 978-0-949683-45-8
www.margaretbrandman.com

**ORDER NUMBER MMP 8081**
International copyright secured (APRA/AMCOS). All rights reserved.

Unauthorised reproduction of any part of this publication by any means,
including photocopying, is an infringement of copyright.

## Acknowledgements

My sincere thanks to:

Anna Hirst for formative work on the project.
Don Ezard for the Illustrations.
Gabrielle Tydd at *Jelly Design* for
specialist advice and final production.


Typesetting, layout and design by Margaret Brandman

# Introduction

*Harmony Comes Together* is designed to equip the student with the necessary skills to write both four-part and three-part classical harmony and to cross the divide between contemporary popular, jazz and contemporary classical writing styles with ease and understanding, all the while giving experience in skills required for both classical and contemporary examination syllabi. This harmony method is the part of an integrated course which provides materials for ear-training (audio and workbooks), theory, improvisation, technique and repertoire.

*Harmony Comes Together* is best used upon completion of both
the *Contemporary Theory Workbook*— Book 2 and the first section
of the *Contemporary Chord Workbook*— Book One.

**Key features of this book are:**

- **gestalt approach**
  — using the gestalt (whole) view of the topic of harmony, students are equipped to see, hear and understand the chords in context

- the emphasis on the understanding of the **cycle of fifths** and **chord tables**

- the understanding of **root progressions** which:
  a) helps the student of harmony make connections between various progressions and the movement of the parts
  b) imparts the knowledge of the effect of the progressions: static, weak or strong

- the use of **colour coding** and **graphics** to impart concepts and illustrate ideas

- the use of various types of labelling from both the British System and the American system, so that information in this book can be used with multiple examination syllabi

- the use of both traditional system of **figuring for chords** and **modern chord symbols** to make the link between old and new systems of music notation and harmonic understanding.

- the awareness of **sounds** in both classical and popular music

- encouragement for the student **to play and listen to** the progressions and to interpret them with modern rhythms

For more detailed information refer to the website:
www.margaretbrandman.com

**Margaret Brandman**
Ph.D. (Mus/Arts )., B.Mus.,
T.Mus.A., Hon.FNMSM.,
F.Mus.Ed.ASMC., F.Comp.ASMC.,
L.Perf.ASMC., A.Mus.A., ASA. T.Dip

*International Woman of the Year* for services to music 2003
awarded by the International Biographical Centre, Cambridge. UK

# Contents

| Topic | Page |
|---|---|
| Comparison of current practice in harmony | ....6 |
| **Cycle of Fifths** | ....7 |
| **Scale and Chord Review** Scale-tone triads built on notes of the major scale | ....8 |
| **Major key 'Chord Table'** | ....9 |
| **Minor scale and chord review** Scale-tone triads built on notes of the minor scale | ....10 |
| **Minor key 'Chord Table'** | ....11 |
| Four-part harmony Vocal ranges & spacing | ....12 |
| **Four-part settings of the root-position chord** | ....13 |
| Six settings of the 'usual' voicing | ....14 |
| Harmony Comes Together—Voicing Exercise Root-position chords in six settings | ....15 |
| Harmony Comes Together—Ready Reference Page: Questions on the *Cycle of Fifths* & *Chord Tables* | ....16 |
| Procedure for writing chords in four-part harmony Questions on root-pos. chords in four parts | ....17 |
| More questions on root-pos. chords in four parts | ....18 |
| Inversions of chords Questions: Three-note chords in close position | ....19 |
| **First-inversion chords in four parts** | ....20 |
| Set-up moves for first-inversion chords | ....21 |
| More questions on first-inversion chords in four parts | ....22 |
| Second-inversion chords in close position | ....23 |
| **Second-inversion chords in four parts** | ....24 |
| Questions on second-inversion chords in four parts | ....25 |
| Summary of settings (usual form), Harmony in Action! | ....26 |
| **Writing Harmony in Piano Style** | ....27 |
| **Harmonic progressions** — General aims | ....28 |
| **Sounds to Avoid in Traditional Four-Part Harmony** *Sounds to avoid:* 1) Consecutive P8 and P5 | ....29 |
| How to check for consecutive P8's and P5's | ....30 |
| Consecutive P5's and P8's - Search and Rescue | ....31 |
| *Sounds to avoid:* 2) Exposed P5's and P8's | ....32 |
| *Sounds to avoid:* 3) Overlapping 4) False relation | ....33 |
| *Sounds to avoid:* 5) Aug 2 & Aug 4 in a melodic line | ....34 |
| *Sounds to avoid:* 6) Doubled 3rd in a major chord | ....35 |
| **Root Progressions – Part 1:** Primes (Same chords) | ....36 |
| Procedure & Questions: Root Prog. – Part 1 | ....37 |
| **Root Progressions – Part 2A: 3↑ – 6↓** | ....38 |
| Questions: Part Two A (3↑ – 6↓) in Root Pos. | ....39 |
| Questions: Part Two A(3↑ – 6↓) Mixing root pos. & first inv. chords | ....40 |
| **Root Progressions – Part Two B: 3↓ – 6↑** | ....41 |
| Questions: Part Two B (3↓ – 6↑) Mixing root pos. & first inv. chords | ....42 |
| More Questions: Part Two B (3↓ – 6↑) | ....43 |
| **Root Progressions – Part Three A: 4↑ – 5↓** | ....44 |
| Questions: Part Three A (4↑ – 5↓) in root pos. | ....45 |
| Root Progressions Part Three A¹ (4↑ – 5↓) with *falling* soprano melody lines | ....46 |
| More Questions: Part Three A: (4↑ – 5↓) | ....47 |
| More Questions: Part Three A(4↑ – 5↓) and extended progressions | ....48 |
| Sequences using Falling Fifths (Rising Fourths) | ....49 |
| 'Cycle of Fifths' progressions | ....50 |
| Transposition — 'Cycle of Fifths' progressions | ....51 |
| **Root Progressions – Part Three B: 4↓ – 5↑** | ....52 |
| Questions: Part Three B (4↓ – 5↑) in root pos. | ....53 |
| Questions: Part Three B (4↓ – 5↑) Mixing root pos. & first inv. chords | ....54 |
| More Questions: Part Three B: 4↓ – 5↑ | ....55 |
| **Root Progressions – Part Four A: 2↑ – 7↓** | ....56 |
| The V-vi; V-VI progression | ....57 |
| Questions: Part Four A(2↑– 7↓) in root position | ....58 |
| More Questions: Part Four A(2↑– 7↓) Mixing root pos. & first inv. chords | ....59 |
| **Root Progressions – Part Four B: 2↓ – 7↑** | ....60 |
| The **vi -V; VI-V** progression | ....61 |
| Questions: Part Four B(2↓–7↑) in root position Harmony Comes Together, Extended Progression | ....62 |
| Questions: Part Four B(2↓–7↑) Mixing root pos. & first inv. chords | ....63 |
| A series of first inv. chords (major key) | ....64 |
| Common progressions using **three** chords | ....65 |

| Topic | Page | Topic | Page |
|---|---|---|---|
| **Root Progressions – Part 5:** | | Plagal Cadence IV-I, iv-i | ....82 |
| Root Progressions in *Action* Question 1—major key | ....66 | Perfect (Authentic) Cadence with a Plagal extension | ....83 |
| Root Progressions in *Action* Questions 2 & 3 — major key | ....67 | **Imperfect Cadence (Semicadence)** | ....84 |
| Root Progressions in *Action* Summary of Root Pos.& First Inv. Chords. Readily available in Major &Minor keys Question 4 — major key Question 5 — major key | ....68 | Four types of Imperfect Cadence (Semicadence) I—V. i—V ii—V IV—V, iv —V vi —V, VI—V | ....85 |
| Root Progressions in *Action* Play, Listen to & Analyse Chorales in Minor Keys Questions 6, 7, 8 — minor key | ....69 | **Interrupted Cadence V-vi, (V-VI) (Deceptive Cadence)** | ....86 |
| Root Progressions in *Action* Chord Progressions in minor keys Questions 9, 10, 11— minor key | ....70 | Precadential chords and Pre-dominant chords | ....87 |
| Harmony Comes Together *Aura Lee*—version one Applied analysis using Root Pos. & First Inv. chords | ....71 | Questions on cadences with precadential chords | 88-90 |
| Root Progressions—Review exercises Section One — Root-position chords | ....72 | **Longer progressions and the Basics of Two-Part Writing** | ....91 |
| Root Progressions—Review exercises Section Two — Root-position & first inversion chords | ....73 | Guidelines for the harmonisation of a song | ....92 |
| **Cadences** | ....74 | **Harmonisation of 'Portsmouth'** | ....93 |
| More facts about cadences Labelling of cadences | ....75 | **Harmonisation of 'Flow Gently, Sweet Afton'** | ....94 |
| Four types of cadences in Major Keys and Minor Keys | ....76 | Harmonisation of 'Grün, Grün, Grün sind alle meine Kleider' | ....95 |
| Where to use cadences in the phrases of a piece Practical exercises | ....77 | Answer page 1 — *Harmony in Action* from p26 plus 'Portsmouth' from p93 | ....96 |
| **Perfect Cadence (Authentic Cadence) V-I , (V-i)** | ....78 | Answer page 2 — 'Flow Gently, Sweet Afton' | ....97 |
| Questions on V-I Cadences (4↑ – 5↓) | ....79 | Answer page 3 — 'Grün, Grün, Grün sind alle meine Kleider' | ....98 |
| Part Two—Resolution of a V-I Cadence where the melody falls | ....80 | Preview of *Harmony Comes Together* –Book 2 | ....99 |
| More Questions on V-I Cadences (4↑ – 5↓) | ....81 | Harmony Comes Together—Extra Practice Page | ...100 |

# Comparison of Current Practice in the Approach to Harmony

*This page contains some of the musical items which are labelled differently by texts written in the British tradition or the American tradition.*

### Degree numbers and degree names

- In most books written in the English tradition, *scale degree numbers* are written either as Arabic numbers or as Roman numerals. *Chord degree numbers* are almost always indicated with Roman numerals.
- In some American publications the degree numbers in a melodic context, are indicated with Arabic numerals topped with a *'caret'* ^ , for instance -   $\hat{1}\ \hat{2}\ \hat{3}\ \hat{4}\ \hat{5}\ \hat{6}\ \hat{7}\ \hat{8}$
- In this book, scale degree numbers are written as Arabic numbers without carets. If desired the student may indicate degree numbers using the caret system.
- The 7th degree of the major scale or harmonic minor scale (a *semitone* away from the upper tonic) is labelled **leading note** in British texts, and **leading tone** in texts from the USA.
- If the 7th degree is a *tone* lower than the upper tonic, as found in the natural minor scale and in some modes, in American texts it is sometimes labelled the **subtonic.**

### Cadences

- In the British system there are four types of cadences:

  1) **Perfect** 2) **Plagal** 3) **Imperfect** 4) **Interrupted**
- In some American texts **perfect cadences** are labelled **authentic cadences** and are further subdivided into —

  a) **Perfect Authentic Cadences** (PAC) where the degree numbers for the melody move 2—1 or 7 –1.

  b) **Imperfect Authentic Cadences** (IAC) where the soprano melody finishes on 5 or 3.
- The **imperfect cadence** (British) is labelled **semi-cadence** in some American texts.
- The **interrupted cadence** is known by several other names including *surprise, deceptive and abrupt.* See page 75 of this book for details.
- Cadences which include one chord in an inversion are sometimes labelled **medial** cadences.
- The terms **full close** and **half close** are also found in reference to final and intermediary cadences in both British and American texts.

### Decorative notes

- **Passing notes** — this term is used in both British and American systems.
- Upper and lower **auxiliary** notes — found in the British system, are described as upper and lower **neighbors** *(American Spelling)* in American texts.

### Scale terminology

- Tonic minor scales — British
- Parallel minor scales — American

  These are terms for minor scales which begin on the *same tonic* as their corresponding major scales.

# Cycle of Fifths

Here is the **Cycle of Fifths** (also known as **Circle of Fifths**) showing the **major keys** on the outer circle and the **relative minor keys** in the middle circle. The keys to the right move *up* by fifths — the keys to the left move *down* by fifths. The numbers on the inner circle indicate the number of sharps or flats for each pair of keys. The key signatures for all keys up to seven sharps and seven flats are presented below the cycle.

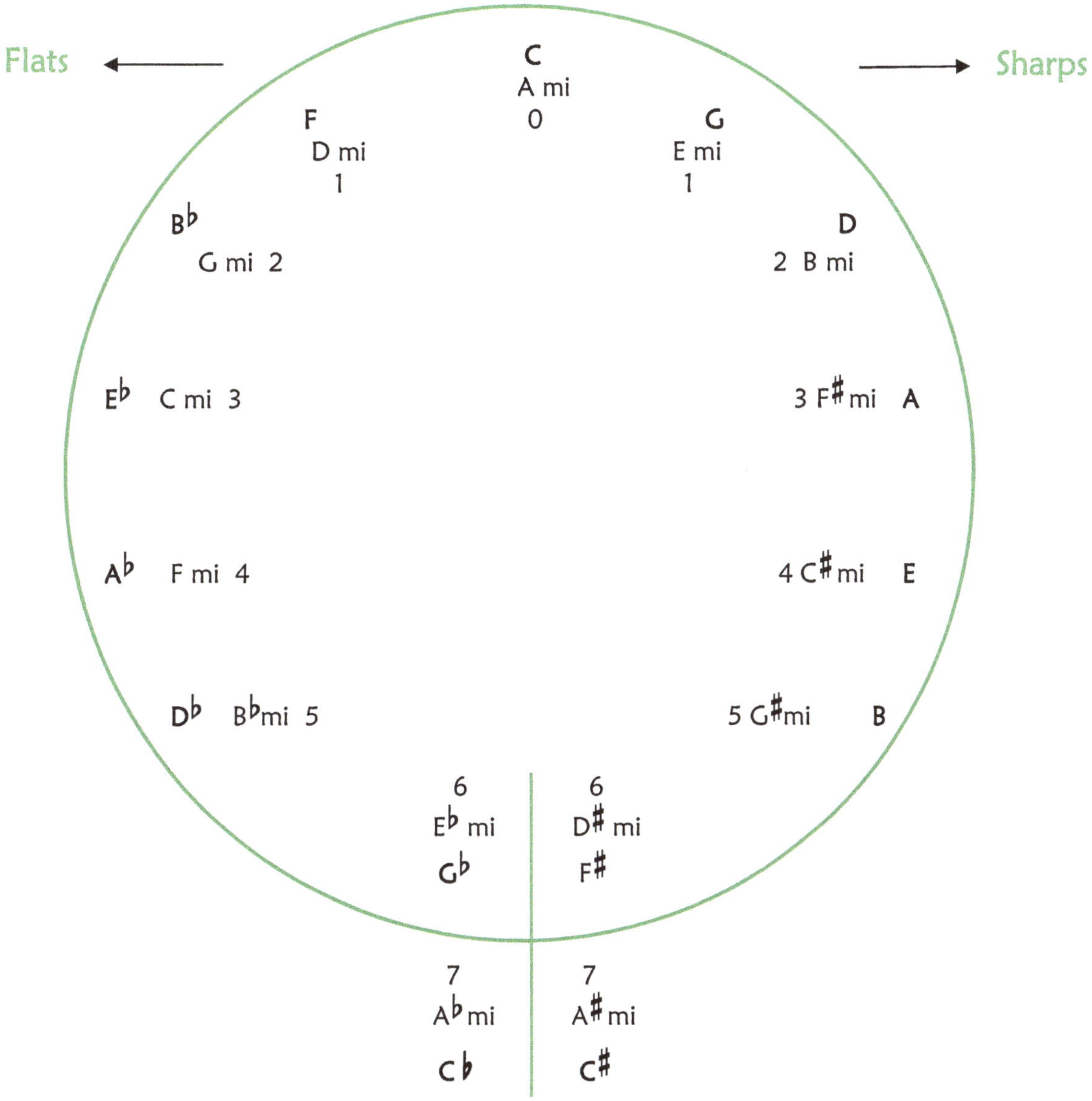

Flats ←　　　　　　　　　　　　　　　　　　　　　　　　→ Sharps

```
                        C
                       A mi
              F          0         G
             D mi                 E mi
              1                    1
      B♭                                    D
         G mi  2                      2  B mi

  E♭  C mi  3                              3  F#mi  A


  A♭   F mi  4                             4  C#mi  E


     D♭  B♭mi  5                        5  G#mi    B
                    6           6
                   E♭ mi      D#mi
                    G♭          F#

                    7           7
                   A♭mi        A#mi
                    C♭          C#
```

The Seven Sharps in Key Signature Sequence　　　　The Seven Flats in Key Signature Sequence

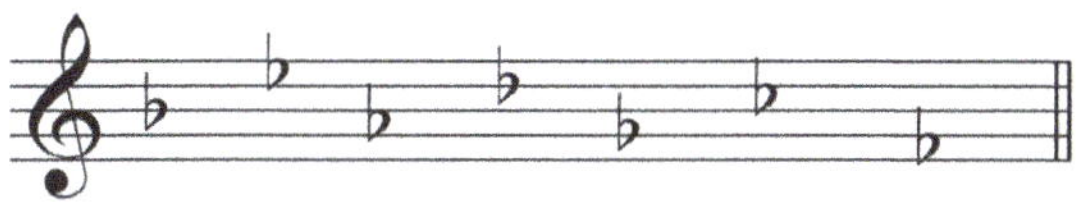

# Scale and Chord Review

**Prerequisite for this page:**
*Contemporary Theory Workbook — Book 2:* Lessons 23-26
*Contemporary Chord Workbook— Book 1:* Pages 1-19

## FIVE TYPES OF TRIAD
*Major, Minor, Diminished, Augmented and Suspended Fourth*

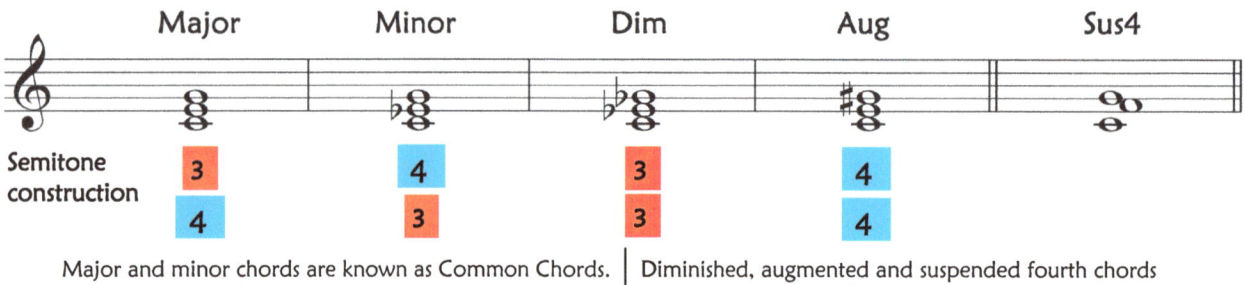

Major and minor chords are known as Common Chords. They can be used as *rest* chords at the end of a section, as well as active chords during a piece.

Diminished, augmented and suspended fourth chords are *leading function* chords used in the body of a piece.

## Question One
- Write these triads in **root position** using accidentals.

E♭    Dm    Asus4    F+    B°    Gmi

## Question Two
### Scale-Tone Triads in the Major Scale
a) Write the chord symbols for each triad built on the scale degrees of **D major scale.**
b) Write the degree numbers. Use *upper case* roman numerals for **major & augmented** chords. E.g. **IV** Use *lower case* roman numerals for **minor** and **diminished** chords. E.g. **iii** or **vi**

Chord Symbol  D    Emi    ___    ___    ___    ___    ___    ___

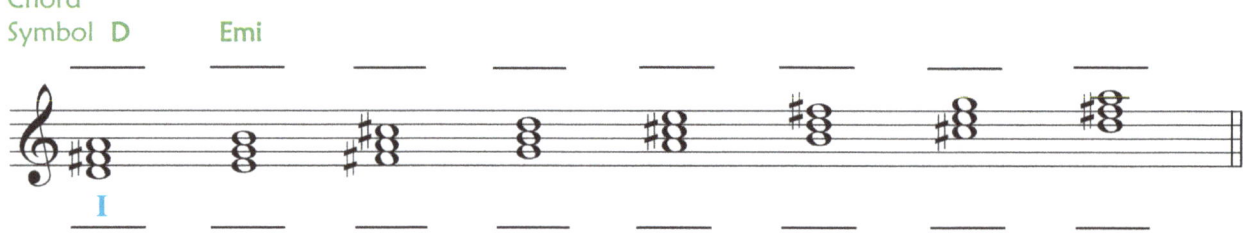

I    ___    ___    ___    ___    ___    ___    ___

Degree numbers

## Question Three
- On which degrees did the **major chords** occur in Question 2?  ____  ____  ____

## Question Four
- On which degrees did the **minor chords** occur in Question 2?  ____  ____  ____

## Question Five
- On which degrees did the **diminished chord** occur in Question 2?  ____

# The Major Key 'Chord Table'

The chords of the **major scale** can be laid out in a table which shows their connections to the Cycle of Fifths and the relationship of each major chord to its relative minor chord.

*For a full explanation refer to Page 18 of Contemporary Chord Workbook 1.*

Notice the **relative minor** chords placed under the major chords. These chords can be used to substitute for one another in a progression. *More on this topic later...*

EXAMPLE:  Chord Table for the Key of C Major

| IV | I | V |
|---|---|---|
| F | C | G |
| ii | vi | iii |
| Dm | Am | Em |
|  |  | vii° |
|  |  | B° |

## Question Six
- Fill in the letter names for each degree of the scale of A major.

**A Major Chord Table**

| IV | I | V |
|---|---|---|
|  |  |  |
| ii | vi | iii |
|  |  |  |
|  |  | vii° |

## Question Seven
- Write full chord tables — degree numbers and chord symbols, for the keys of B♭ major and E major.

**B♭ Major Chord Table**

**E Major Chord Table**

# Minor Scale and Chord Review

**Scale-Tone Triads in the Minor Scale**

**Question One**
- Supply the **chord symbol** and **degree number** for each of the triads built on the three forms of the minor scale.
- Draw a coloured box around the most frequently used chord type on each degree in the varying forms of the minor scale. Use a different colour for each one. See the example that has been done for chord **ii**.

Natural Minor and Descending Melodic Minor

CHORD SYMBOL ___ ___ ___ ___ ___ ___ ___ ___

DEGREE ___ ___ ___ ___ ___ ___ ___ ___

Harmonic Minor

CHORD SYMBOL ___ ___ ___ ___ ___ ___ ___ ___

DEGREE ___ ___ ___ ___ ___ ___ ___ ___

Melodic Minor ascending

CHORD SYMBOL ___ ___ ___ ___ ___ ___ ___ ___

DEGREE ___ ___ ___ ___ ___ ___ ___ ___

---

**Question Two: Collate your information — natural minor & desc. melodic minor**

On which degree did the **minor** chords occur? ___ ___ ___

On which degree did the **major** chords occur? ___ ___ ___

On which degree did the **diminished** chord occur? ___

---

**Question Three: Collate your information — harmonic minor scale**

On which degree did the **minor** chords occur? ___ ___

On which degree did the **major** chords occur? ___ ___

On which degree did the **diminished** chords occur? ___ ___

On which degree did the **augmented** chord occur? ___

---

**Question Four: Collate your information — ascending melodic minor**

On which degree did the **minor** chords occur? ___ ___

On which degree did the **major** chords occur? ___ ___

On which degree did the **diminished** chords occur? ___ ___

On which degree did the **augmented** chord occur? ___

# The Minor Key 'Chord Table'

Notice that the letter names for the table are taken from the **harmonic minor scale**. However the chord types chosen for the table are the most frequently used chords in a minor key. The bracket indicates that the type of chord is used in **both** forms just as frequently. Notice the **relative major chords** placed under the **minor** chords. For a full explanation refer to page 18 of the *Contemporary Chord Workbook – Bk 1*.

EXAMPLE:   Chord Table for the Key of C Minor

|  |  |  |
|---|---|---|
| iv | i | V |
| Fm | Cm | G |
| VI | III$^{(+)}$ | ii$^{o}$ |
| A♭ | E♭ $^{(+)}$ | D$^{o}$ |
|  |  | vii$^{o}$ |
|  |  | B$^{o}$ |

Compare the chords found in this C minor Chord Table to the scale-tone triads that were boxed on page 10.

---

## Question Five

- Fill in the letter names for the chord types for the keys of F minor and B minor.

F Minor Chord Table

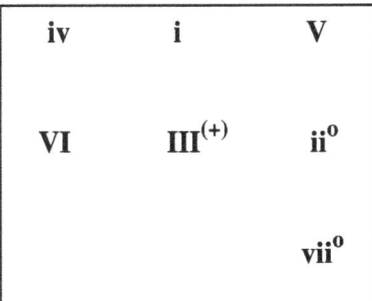

B Minor Chord Table

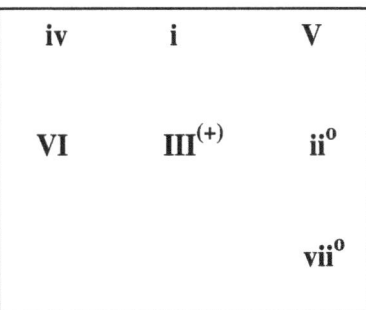

| EXAMPLE OF A MINOR KEY 'CHORD TABLE' INCLUDING LESS FREQUENTLY USED CHORD TYPES |
|---|
| See the brackets for the other possibilities. |
| Keep these chords in mind when harmonising melody notes derived from the melodic minor scale. |

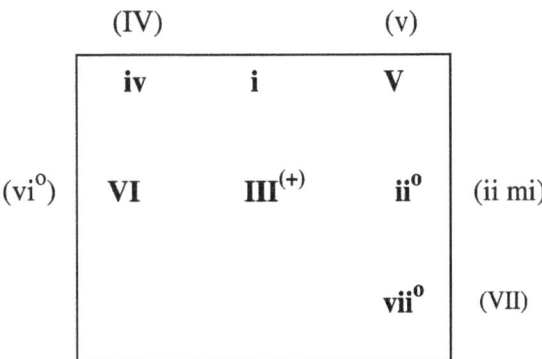

# Four-Part Harmony

 Four-part harmony is the style of writing in which the notes of a chord are assigned to one of each of the four singing voices. SATB : Soprano, Alto, Tenor, Bass.

To begin with, we will use the triads covered on the previous pages, but as they need to be set out for four voices, one of the notes will need to be **'doubled'** that is: used twice.

F major root-position chord
with the 1st degree doubled

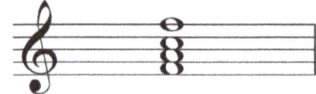

## Vocal Ranges

Four-part settings for voices need to be written within the usual singing range of each type of male or female voice. Stem direction: high voices — up, low voices — down.

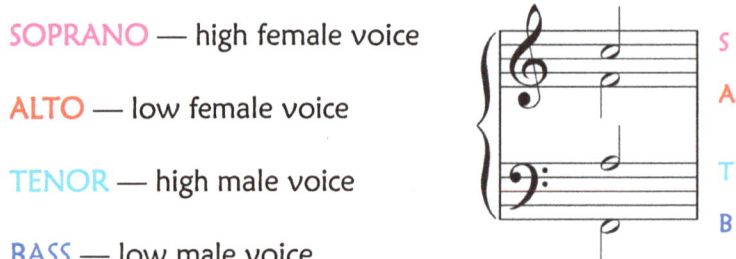

SOPRANO — high female voice

ALTO — low female voice

TENOR — high male voice

BASS — low male voice

STANDARD VOCAL RANGES ( these can be extended by trained singers)

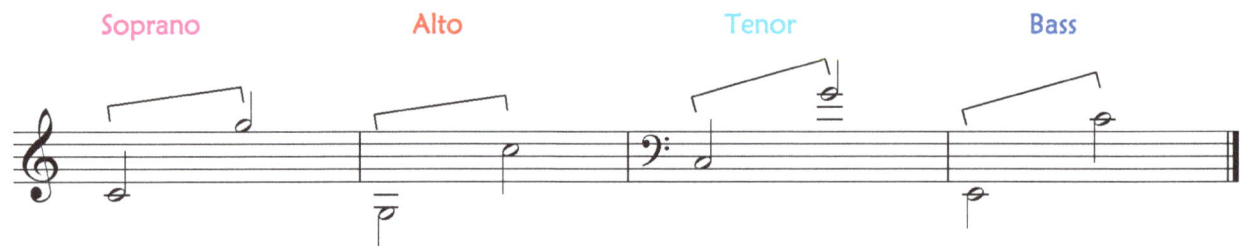

## Spacing

To keep the sound balanced, the interval between each of the upper three notes should be a *simple interval*, an octave or less in size. Any interval, simple or compound, (smaller or larger than the octave) is acceptable between the bass and tenor parts.

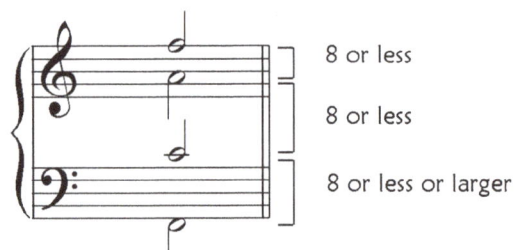

8 or less

8 or less

8 or less or larger

**Special Note**
*In some British harmony books the lowest recommended note for the bass range is F on the space below the staff.
However, the bass range in the Bach Chorales often extends to E as shown in the example above. Therefore this is the recommended range for students using* **Harmony Comes Together**
*(See Bach Chorales 242, 270 & 318).*

# Four-Part Settings of the Root-Position Chord

- There are **four** main ways in which to arrange the notes of a **root-position** major or minor chord.

- Each setting doubles a different degree of the chord.
  (The diminished chord is rarely used in root position owing to its harsh sound.
  It may be used in special cases which will be discussed later in this series.)

- The most common setting is the **'usual'** setting.

- If for some reason this setting does not fit smoothly into a progression of chords then various optional settings are available; they are presented in order of priority.

- You can call them **'emergency'** voicings, as they would be suitable for use when the progression proves problematical or troublesome.
  Doubling the **major third degree** causes the chord to sound somewhat harsh owing to the fact that the major third degree is a strong harmonic in the naturally occurring *harmonic series*. Keen ears can detect this harmonic when the chord is sounded, as it is already present in the chord even if only the first and fifth degrees are sounded. This is why the setting is used sparingly.

- Each setting is a **root-position** chord, as the root is in the bass voice.

- The upper three notes can be placed in any of the three voices at random.

- To remember the colour-coding, think of the meaning of the colours in a traffic light— with an extra colour!

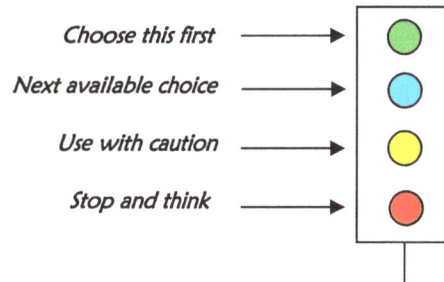

Choose this first → (green)
Next available choice → (blue)
Use with caution → (yellow)
Stop and think → (red)

| Usual | Emergency 1 | Emergency 2 | Emergency 3 |
|---|---|---|---|
| 1 x 5th | 2 x 5th | - | 1 x 5th |
| 1 x 3rd | 1 x 3rd | 1 x 3rd | 2 x 3rd |
| 2 x 1st | 1 x 1st | 3 x 1st | 1 x 1st |
| *A very full sounding setting. First choice in most cases. | *Readily available but slightly thinner sound. Used to reduce big gaps. *Think of this as a smoothing iron!* | *Used in special circumstances. | *Not the best in a major chord but used in special circumstances. OK for a minor chord. |

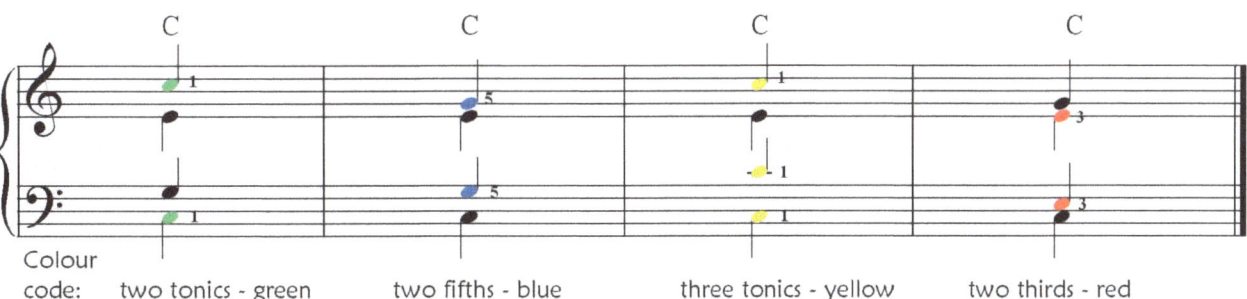

Colour code: two tonics - green | two fifths - blue | three tonics - yellow | two thirds - red

> Special note: there is one even rarer setting that uses a doubled root and a doubled third.
> It can be found in the Bach Chorales from time to time when the voice leading requires this setting.

# Six Settings of the 'Usual' Voicing

| Usual | |
|---|---|
| 1 x 5th | ♩ |
| 1 x 3rd | ♩ |
| 2 x 1st | ♩ ♩ |

There are *six* settings possible when a chord is voiced with a doubled root note.
- They are indicated here by the letters **'a'** to **'f'**.
- The only variations may be when one or more of the notes is displaced by an octave.
- *Close voicing* - the tenor and soprano voices are *within an octave of each other*.
- *Open voicing* - the tenor and soprano voices are *more than an octave apart*.

---

Six Settings - the tenor notes have been blacked in to show the use of the degrees.
- Write the degree numbers next to each of the notes to discover the pattern.

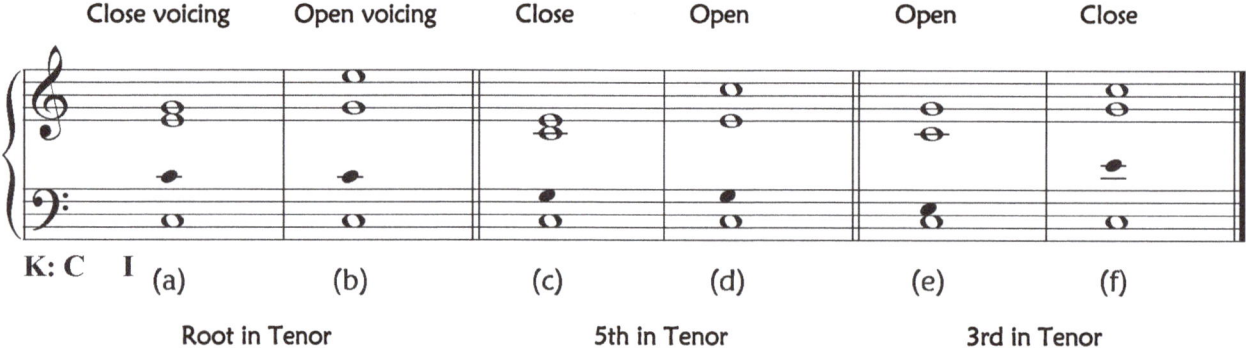

### The Same Voicings with Octave Displacements
- This is only possible if the notes fit within the voice range.

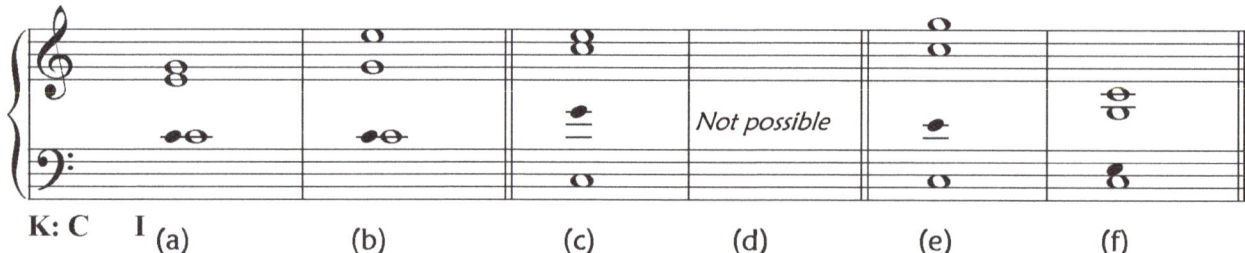

### An Example with Stems Written Correctly for Four-Part Voicings
- Write the degree numbers next to each of the **alto** and **soprano** notes
- Discover the positions of the doubled root notes by colour-coding them green.

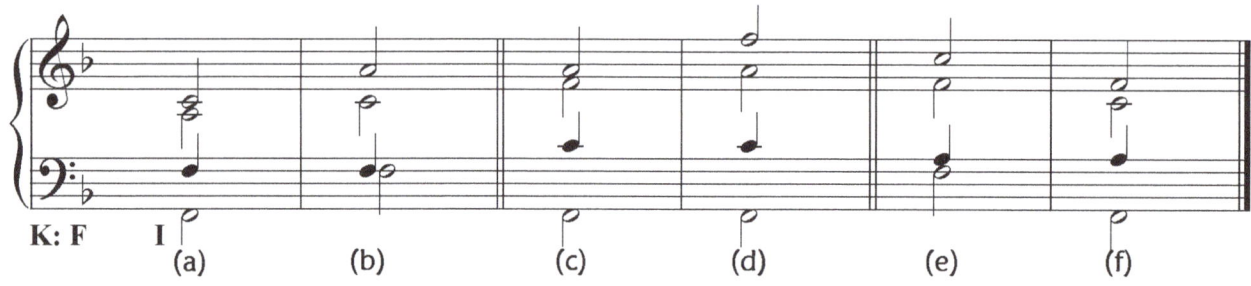

# Harmony Comes Together – Voicing Exercise

Write six settings of these chords, following the models on the previous page:

- Write the chord name above the first bar.
- Write the chords using half notes (minims).
- Take care to use the correct stem direction for each voice.
- Write the degree numbers next to the notes of each chord.
- Colour-code the doubled root notes green.

*As you progress through this book, play and listen to all the examples given and those you write for yourself, to discover the effects of voicings and progressions and develop your ability to hear the sounds in the inner ear.*

1)

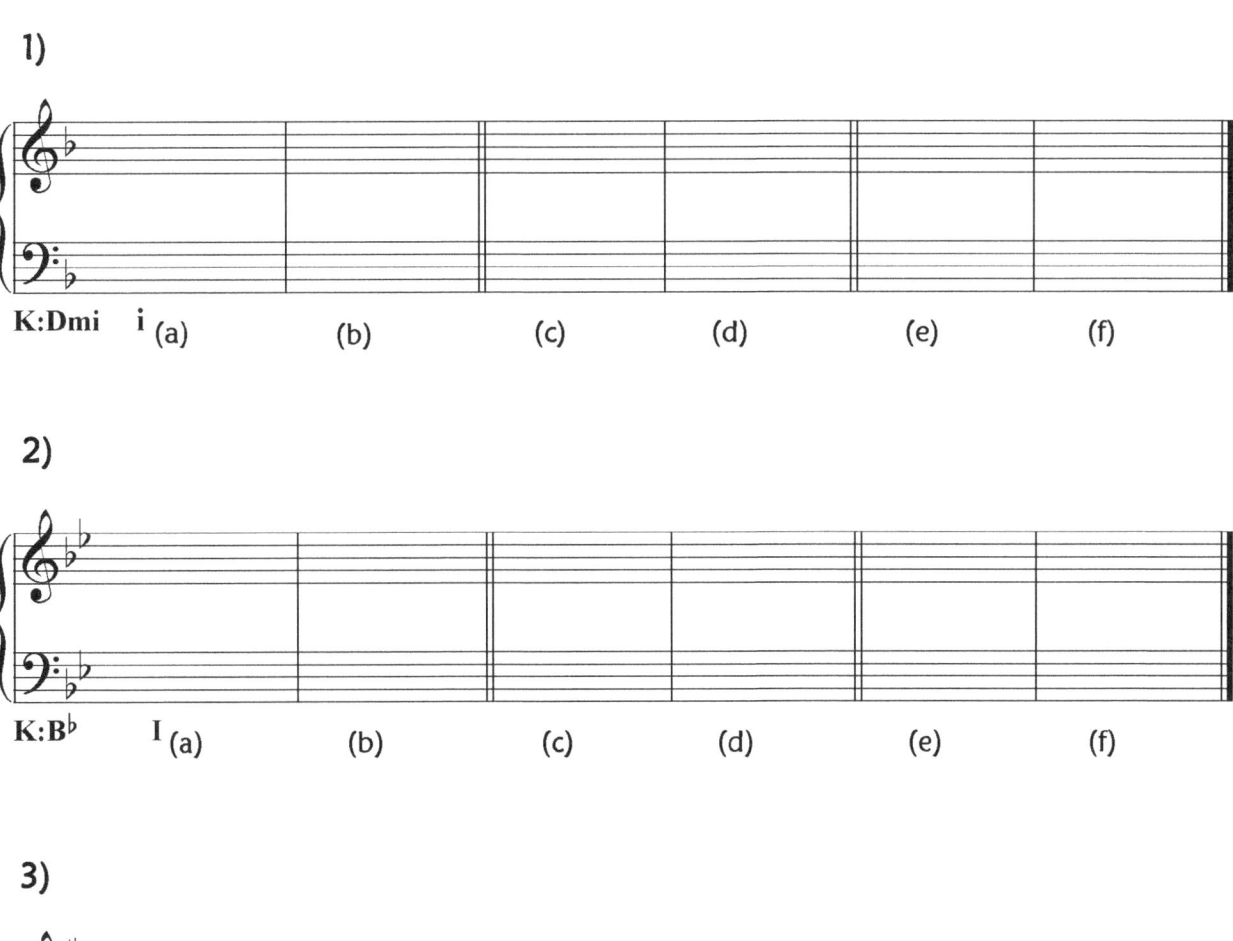

K:Dmi   i  (a)        (b)        (c)        (d)        (e)        (f)

2)

K:B♭   I  (a)        (b)        (c)        (d)        (e)        (f)

3)

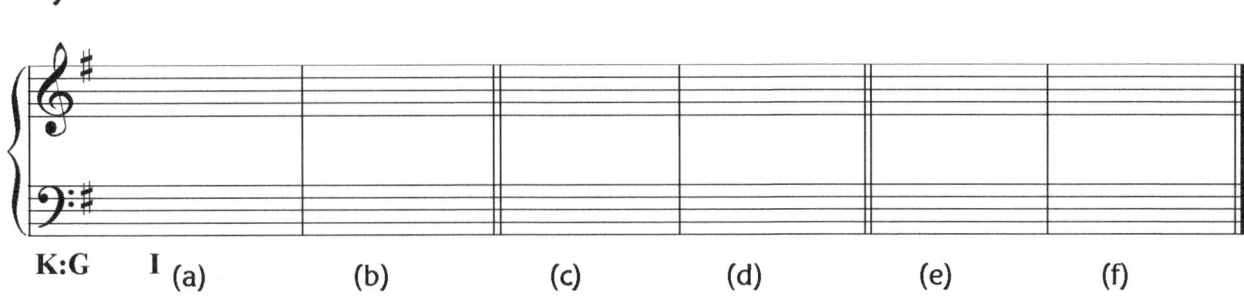

K:G   I  (a)        (b)        (c)        (d)        (e)        (f)

# Harmony Comes Together — Ready Reference Page

Complete these questions and refer to the information as you write the chords on the following pages.

Question One
- Write the Cycle of Fifths including minor keys.

Question Two
- Complete the degree numbers for these chord tables.

| Major Key |
|---|
| I |

| Minor Keys |
|---|
| i |

- Note that the **minor key** 'Chord Table' represents the most frequently used chords in a piece in a minor key. Therefore usually the **dominant triad** will be **major.**
- An accidental is required to raise the seventh degree of the harmonic minor scale, so it leads by semitone to the upper tonic.
- This accidental will apply to the **third degree** of the dominant triad, thereby converting the dominant triad into a major triad.
- Do not double the third degree of the dominant chord, as it is the leading note of the key.
- In the majority of chord progressions — *avoid* doubling the leading note of the key.

# Procedure for Writing Chords in Four–Part Harmony

## SEEING THE WHOLE VIEW

In order to begin writing settings of these root-position major and minor chords you will first need to complete the information required for each chord, referring to the Cycle of Fifths and the Chord Tables to work out your answers.

### SET-UP MOVES
Use these colours —

**G** 1) Supply the **chord symbol** above each chord
(The name is given by the printed bass note)

**O** 2) Supply the **key** in which this is the correct degree

**P** 3) Supply the **type of chord**
e.g. major or minor
For Major - use letter name only and tick to confirm. For minor - '**mi**' (all lower case)

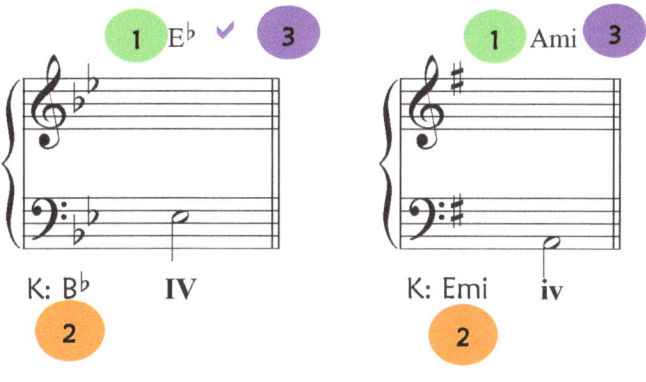

## Questions — Root-Position Chords

*Unless stated otherwise, the required setting for all chords in the following questions will be in four parts. Play each setting once it is written to listen to the effect of the voicing.*

### Question One
- After setting up the information **surrounding** each chord, write one four-part setting of each of these **root-position** chords.
- Vary the voicing using settings (a) to (f) of the **usual** voicing. (2x 1st).
- Remember to raise the *leading tone* in chord **V** in a minor key.
- Finish by colour-coding the doubled root notes. Colour-code them *green.*

### Question Two
- Write another setting of each chord, using the **first emergency voicing** (2x 5th).
(Write them next to the first chord in each bar or on manuscript.)
Colour-code these settings *blue.*

# More Questions on Root-Position Chords in Four Parts

## Question Three

All the chords in this question belong to **major** keys.

Part One:   Set up each chord by providing the key signatures and the chord symbols.

Part Two:   Write root-position chords in the required settings. (See *Six Settings* p14)

Part Three: Colour-code the doubled root notes.

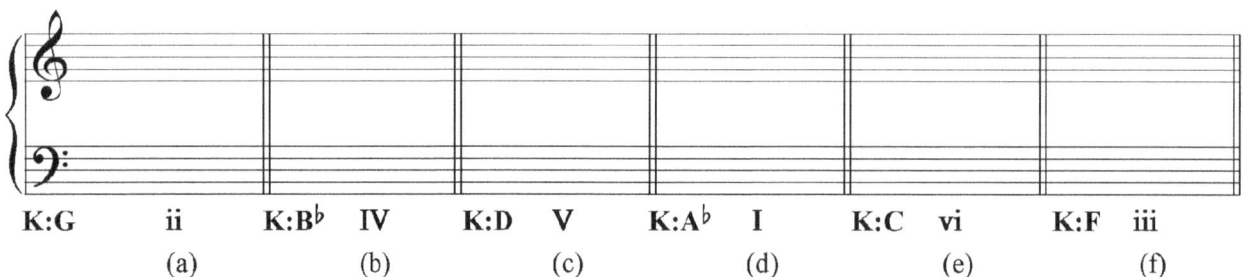

| K:G  ii | K:B♭  IV | K:D  V | K:A♭  I | K:C  vi | K:F  iii |
|---|---|---|---|---|---|
| (a) | (b) | (c) | (d) | (e) | (f) |

## Question Four

Part One:   Identify these **major** keys. (Orange) (1)

Part Two:   Provide the chord symbols for each chord. (Green) (2)

Part Three: Indicate the degree number for each chord. (Dark Blue) (3)

Part Four:  Identify the settings used for each chord. (*a to f*) (4)

Part Five:  Colour-code the doubled root notes.

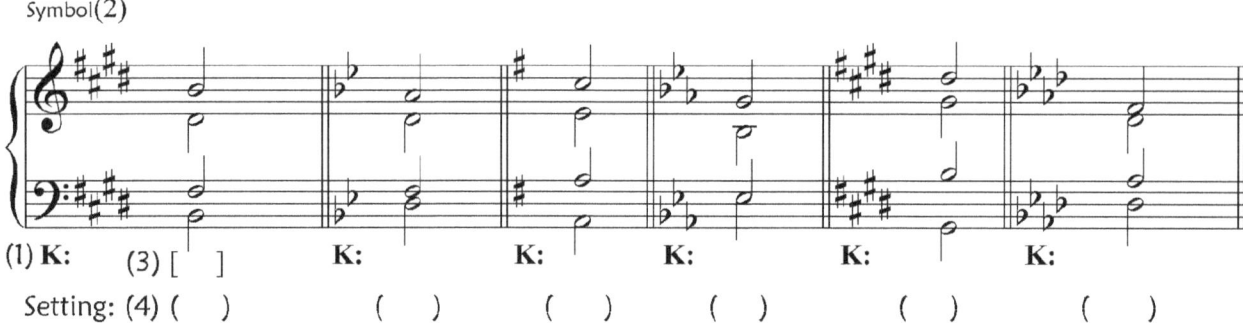

## Question Five

Part One:   Identify these **minor** keys. (Orange)

Part Two:   Provide the chords symbols for each chord. (Green)

Part Three: Indicate the degree number for each chord. (Dark Blue)

Part Four:  Identify the settings used for each chord. (*a to f*)

Part Five:  Colour-code the doubled root notes.

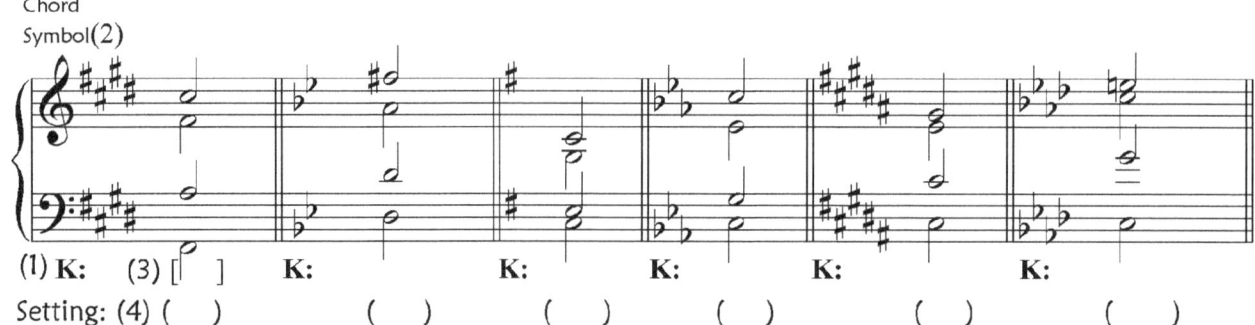

# Inversions of Triads in Close Position

**Any three-note chord (triad) has a root position & two inversions.
The inversions can be indicated by 'figuring'.**

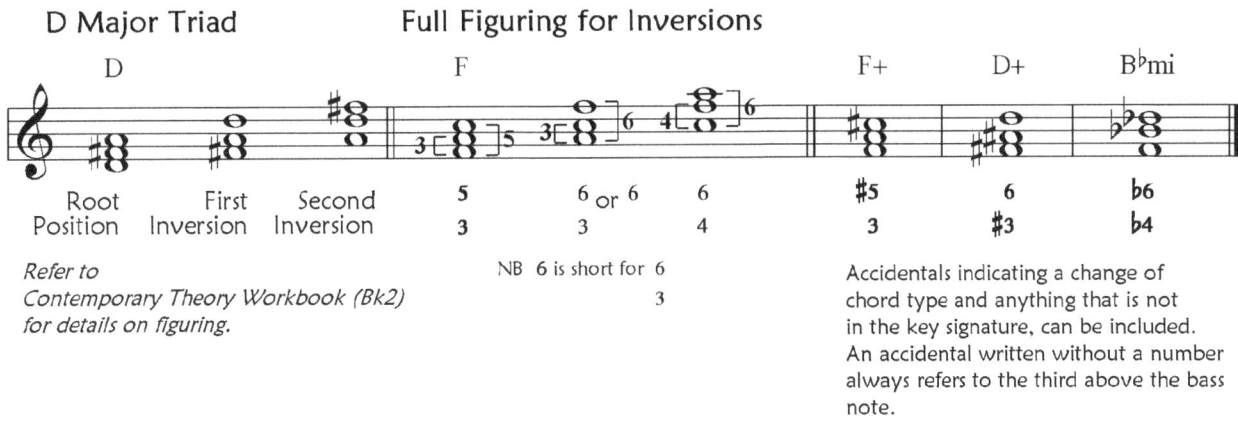

D Major Triad — Root Position, First Inversion, Second Inversion

*Refer to Contemporary Theory Workbook (Bk2) for details on figuring.*

Full Figuring for Inversions

F: 5/3,  6/3 or 6,  6/4

NB 6 is short for 6/3

F+, D+, B♭mi: ♯5/3, 6/♯3, ♭6/♭4

Accidentals indicating a change of chord type and anything that is not in the key signature, can be included. An accidental written without a number always refers to the third above the bass note.

---

 ## Questions — Three-Note Chords in Close Position

1) Write the root position and both inversions of each of these chords.

    G            Cmi          A

2) Supply the chord symbols above the staff and write the figuring (numbers only) for each one below the staff.

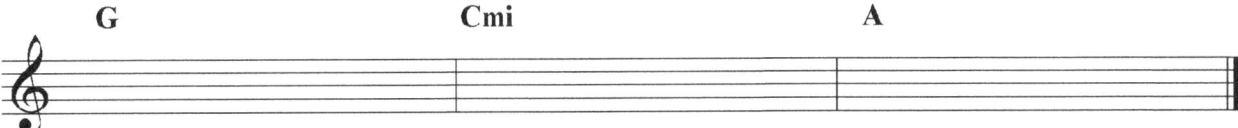

3) Write each of these chords in first inversion.

    Cmi          E♭          F♯         Dmi

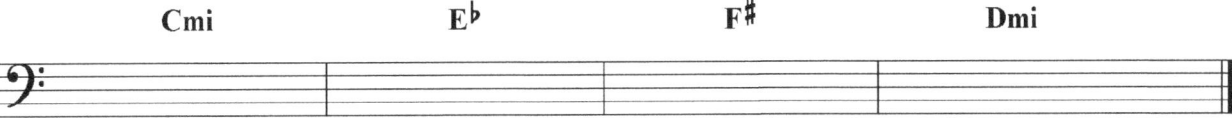

4) Write the full figuring including accidentals, for each of these chords.

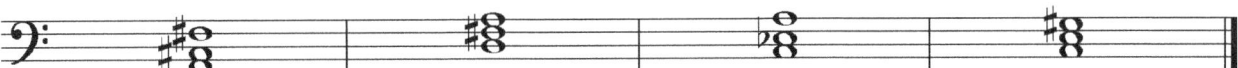

K:C

# First-Inversion Chords in Four Parts

All major, minor and diminished chords are available in first inversion.

The lowest sounding note in a first-inversion chord is the **third** degree of the chord.

---

## Settings of the First-Inversion Chord

There are three ways in which to deal with a **first-inversion** chord.

| Usual | Emergency 1 | Emergency 2 |
|---|---|---|
| 1 x 5th ♩ | 2 x 5th ♩♩ | 1 x 5th ♩ |
| 2x 1st ♩♩ | 1 x 1st ♩ | 1 x 1st ♩ |
| 1 x 3rd ♩ | 1 x 3rd ♩ | 2 x 3rd ♩♩ |

**Sample Settings**
Write the degree numbers next to each note.
Notice the colour-coding of the doubled notes.

> In chord **vii** this voicing is necessary to avoid doubling the leading note.

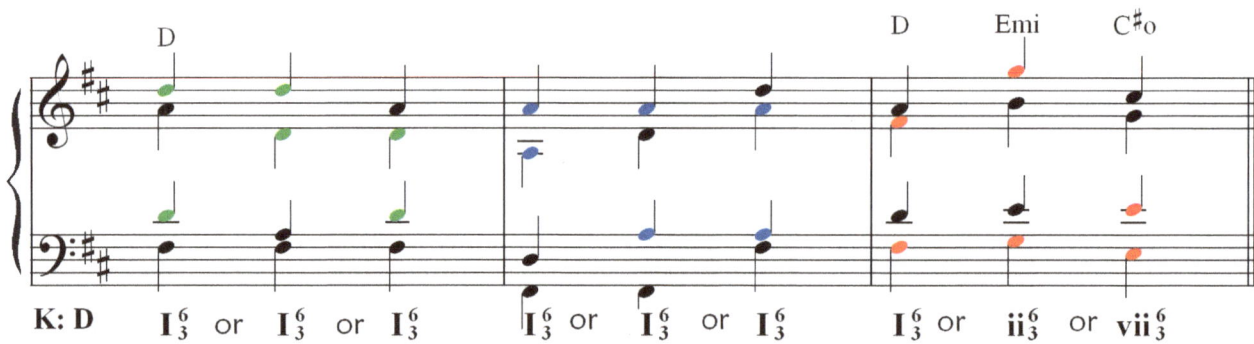

Do not use for a diminished chord. | Emergency for all chord types. | - Not the best for a major chord.
- OK for a minor chord.
- The '**usual**' for a dim chord.

**Voice exchange—the exchange of chord degrees between parts.**

Write the degree numbers next to the notes of both chords in the example below, to see how the root and third degrees have been exchanged.

---

Using *voice-exchange* to convert a root-position triad
to a first-inversion triad

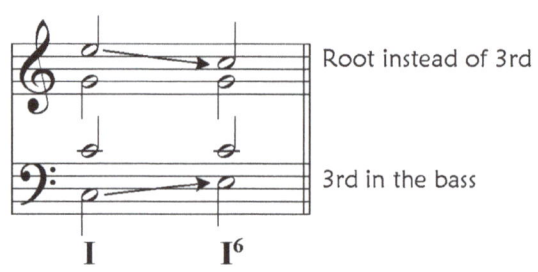

# Set-Up Moves for First-Inversion Chords

In order to begin writing settings of these first-inversion chords you will first
need to complete the information required for each chord.
Refer to the Cycle of Fifths and the Chord Tables to work out your answers. (See p16)

## SET-UP MOVES
Use these colours—

 1) Supply the **chord symbol** above each chord
by locating the Root Note **a third below** the given bass note.

2) Find the **key** to which it belongs

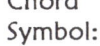 3) Supply the **type of chord** —major, minor or diminished
For diminished chords use a small circle. For instance – D°

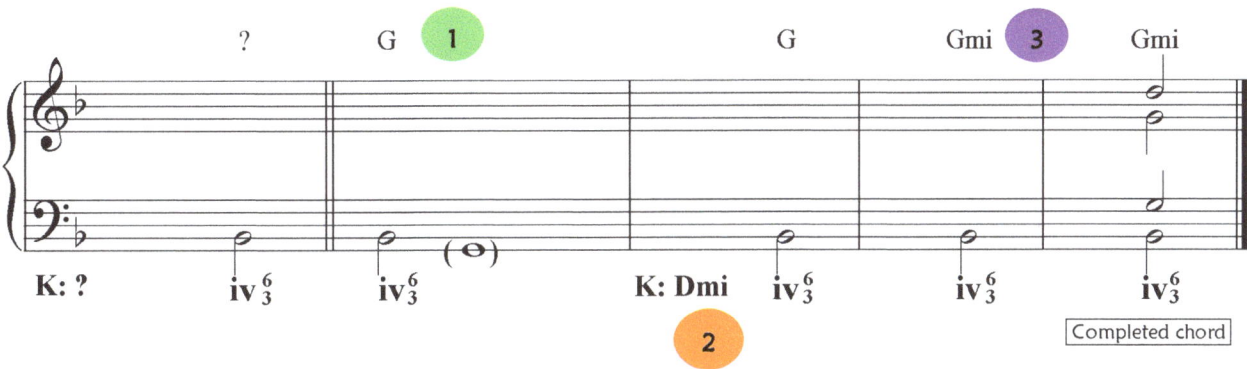

## Question One

- After setting up the information surrounding each chord, (1) - (2) - (3), write
one four-part setting for each chord using the **usual** voicing for *first-inversion* chords.
- Use *Emergency Two* for diminished chords.
- *Remember to raise the leading note in chord V in a minor key.*
- Finish by colour-coding the doubled notes – *green* for roots, *red* for thirds.

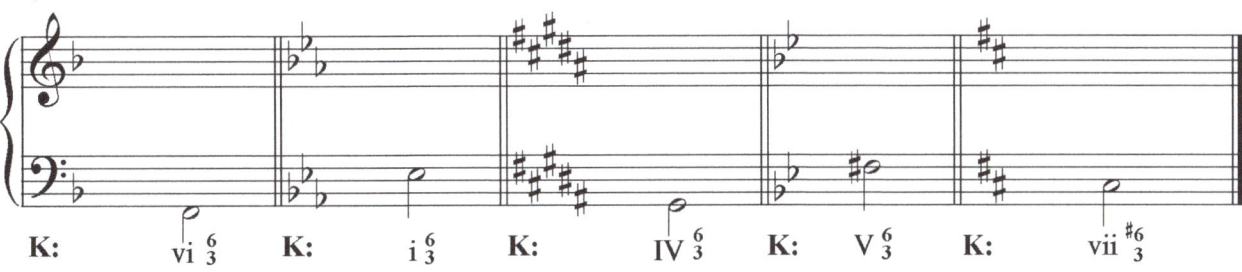

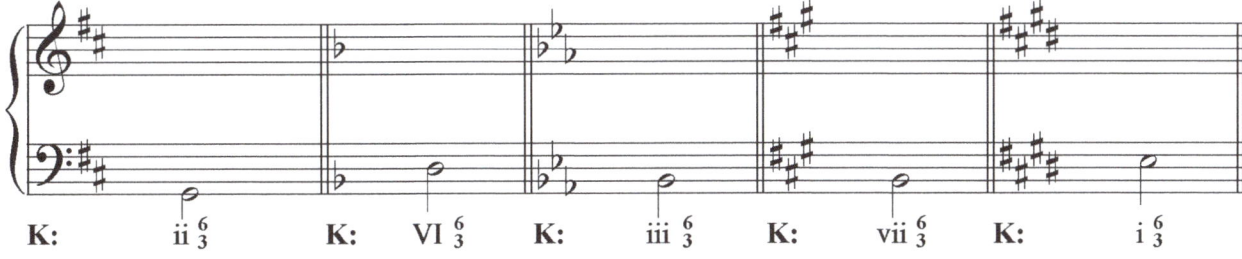

# More Questions on First-Inversion Chords in Four Parts

### Question Two

After setting up the information surrounding each chord, (1) - (2) - (3), write these chords using the optional setting – **emergency one voicing**, for all types of first-inversion chords. *Colour-code the doubled fifths blue.*

### Question Three

Set up each first-inversion chord, providing the key signatures and the chord symbols. Then write it in the required setting: **Usual** or **Emergency One**.

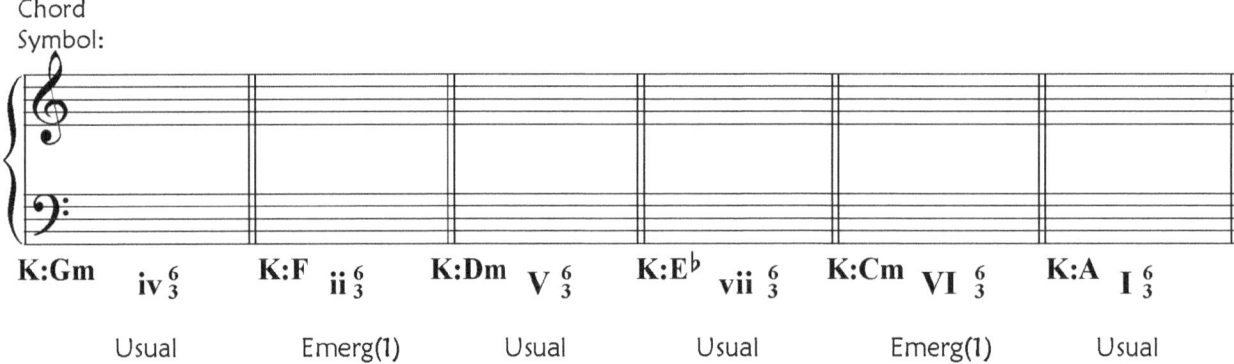

Extra practice staves

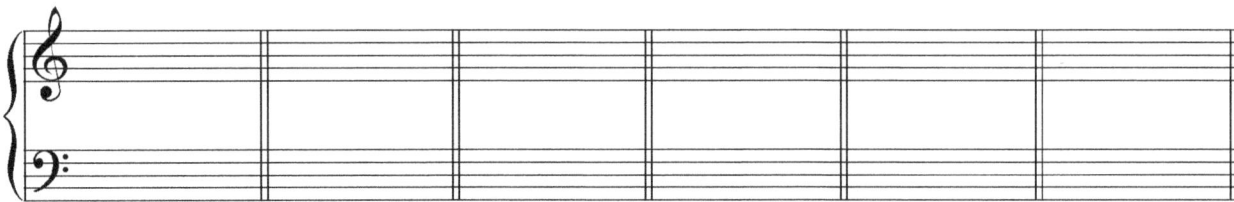

# Second-Inversion Chords in Close Position

 ## Inversion Practice

1) Write the Root Position and both inversions of each of these chords.

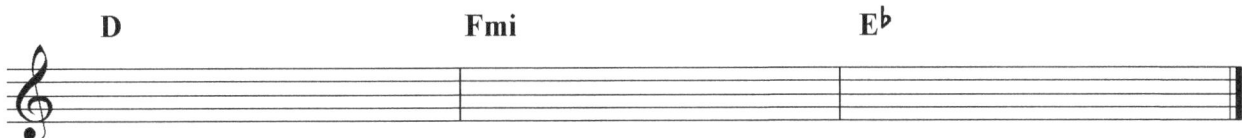

2) Name these chords and write the figuring (numbers only) for each one below the staff.

3) Write each of these chords in second inversion.

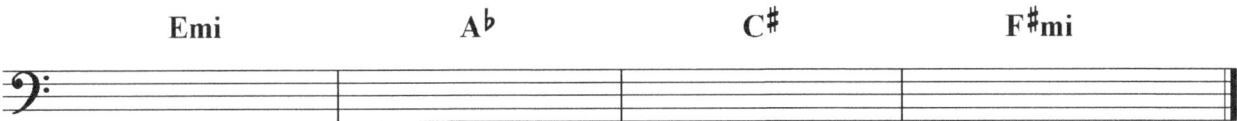

4) Write the full figuring including accidentals, for each of these chords.
   There is no need to supply the accidental for the lowest note of each chord.

K:C

Extra practice staves

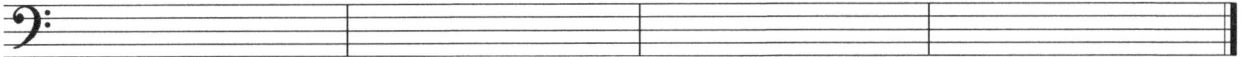

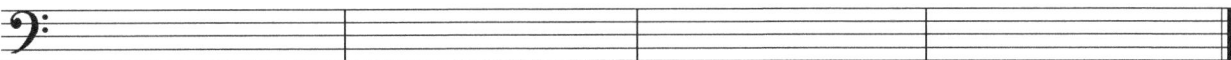

# Second-Inversion Chords in Four Parts

Second-inversion chords are used in specific situations.
The lowest sounding note in a second inversion chord is the *fifth* of the chord.
Their usage will be covered in book two of this series.

## Setting of the Second-Inversion Chord

There is only one combination of voices for a second-inversion chord.

| Usual |
|---|
| 1 x 1st ♩ |
| 1 x 3rd ♩ |
| 2 x 5th ♩♩ |

Second-inversion chords are easy to write.
After placing the fifth degree in the bass part,
simply write one of each of the notes of the triad
above it, in any order.
The result will be a chord with a doubled fifth.

### Sample Settings
Write the degree numbers next to each note.
Notice the colour-coding of the doubled notes.

### Converting a root-position setting to a second-inversion setting —
Just change the bass note!

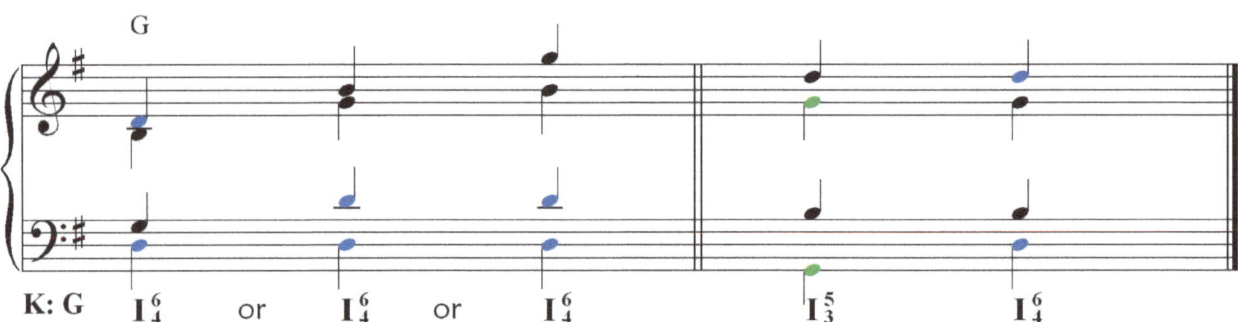

## SET- UP MOVES FOR SECOND-INVERSION CHORDS

Use these colours —

**G**  1) Supply the **chord symbol** above each chord by locating the root note a **fifth** below the given bass note.

**O**  2) Find the **key** to which it belongs

**P**  3) Supply the **type of chord** (major, minor)

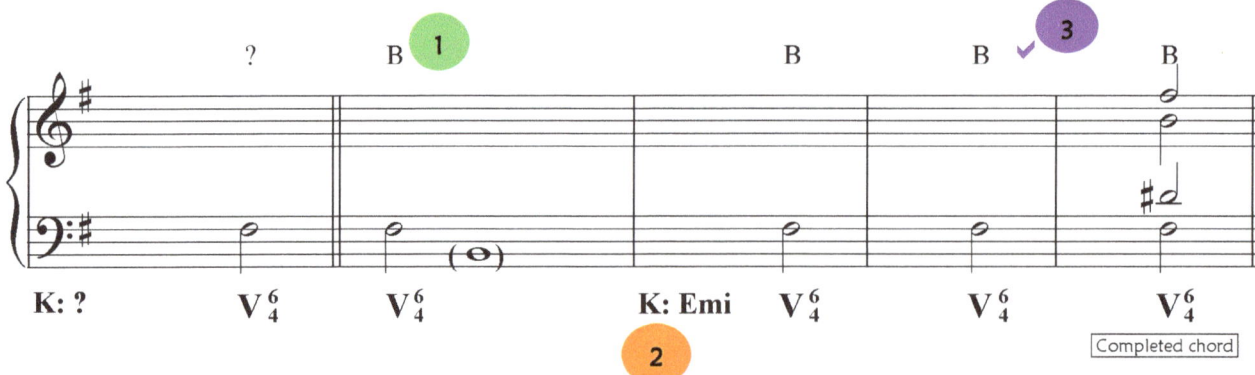

Remember to raise the *leading note*
in the dominant chord in a minor key!

# Questions on Second-Inversion Chords in Four Parts

### Question One

After setting up the information surrounding each chord, (1) - (2) - (3), write four-part settings for each of these **second-inversion** chords.
Colour-code each setting to check for the correct doublings.

### Question Two — review of all chord positions

Supply the chord symbols, the degree numbers and the figuring for these chords in various positions. *For a root-position chord only the degree number needs to be written as the figuring is understood.*
Use dark blue for the degree numbers and figuring.
Colour-code each setting to discover the degree that has been doubled.

# Summary of Settings in the Usual Form

| Root Position | Second Inversion | First Inversion |
|:---:|:---:|:---:|
| 5 | 5 | 1 |
| 3 | 3 | 5 |
| 1 | 1 | 1 |
| [1] | [5] | [3] |

The upper three degrees can be placed in any of the upper voices.
*Colour-code the doublings on the examples below.*

## *Harmony In Action ! — A preview*
### Analysis Exercise — Root, 1st and 2nd Inversion chords

Here is a preview of a completed harmonisation which you will learn to do for yourself as you progress through this book. The harmonisation incorporates chords in different inversions which produces an effective, homogenous sound. As you move further through this book, you will discover the reasons for the use of the emergency voicings.

**Chord Table**

1) Write a chord table for the key
2) Supply the modern chord symbols above the chords
3) Supply the degree numbers and figuring below the staff
4) Colour-code the notes which are doubled in each chord using the standard colours.

*Notice that the doubled fifth can be used to smooth out a line and avoid a large leap.*

*Answers to this exercise appear on page 96.*

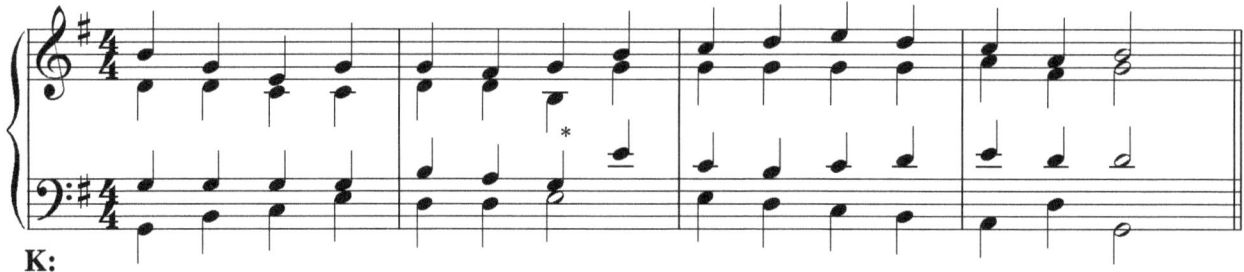

\* See Interrupted (Deceptive) Cadence p86

# Writing Harmony in Piano Style

- When chords are written in piano style, the *upper three parts* are written in the treble stave within the range of the octave hand-span.
- The bass part remains in the bass clef with the stems written in the usual direction for a single line.
- The doubled voices may be written next to each other, or omitted altogether.

Question One — Here is the progression from the previous page written in piano style
- Write the chord names, degree numbers and figuring, then play and listen to it.

K:

### How to Convert a Four-Part Vocal Style Setting into a Piano Style Arrangement

If the four-part setting is in an *open* voicing, **take the tenor part up an octave** and place the note in the treble staff. If the notes are in a *close voicing* simply **move the tenor part into the treble staff at the same pitch**. Attach all three treble notes to the same stem.

Question Two
a) Write a chord table for the key of this piece
b) Analyse this four-part setting as was done on the previous page, then rewrite it in piano style and play it.

K:

\* Bye-tone
Another note of the chord inserted
to avoid consecutive fifths or octaves.

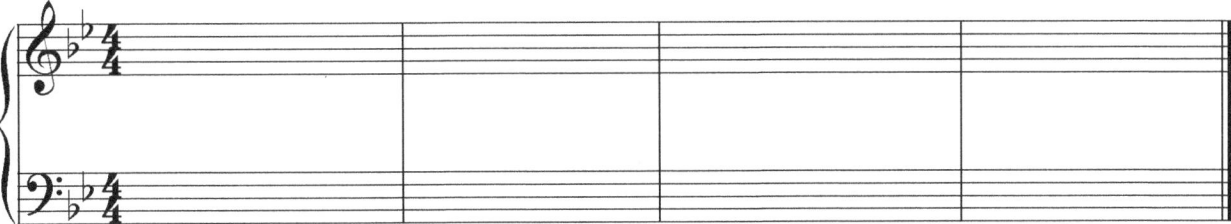

# Harmonic Progressions

> An *harmonic progression* consists of several chords in succession each producing a varied tonal effect.

Here are some general principles although they can be varied occasionally.

## General Aims

Things to aim for when writing two chords in succession:

1) In the upper three parts, keep the movements between the notes in each part **close-by**: using intervals of Same (Prime), Step (2nd) and Skip (3rd) where possible

2) Leave a **common note** in the same voice

3) Aim for **contrary motion** between the outer parts whenever possible

4) Resolve notes which are a **semitone apart** in the scale, e.g. 4→3 or 7→8

5) Write **no more than three chords** with outer parts moving in similar motion.

For example

The graphic below summarises the techniques to aim for and the sounds to avoid, when writing traditional four-part harmony.
Each of the branches of the 'avoid' section of the graphic is explained on the following pages.

# Sounds to Avoid in Traditional Four-Part Harmony

## 1) Consecutive or 'Parallel' – Perfect Octaves and Perfect Fifths

In traditional harmony the bare sound of parallel **perfect octaves (P8's)** and **perfect fifths (P5's)** moving in the same direction, in the same voices, in two consecutive chords, is avoided.

**Play and listen to these perfect intervals.** Notice the open and bare quality of the sound.

These parallel intervals remind us of the sound of early church music, the *Gregorian Chant* in particular. At that time, (c1000AD) they were among the few intervals that were in tune, according to the tuning system of the day, which resulted from studies done on sound by the ancient Greek mathematician Pythagoras. In ancient times these intervals were used primarily for harmonized choral singing accompanied by the organ. The accompanying organ was restricted to only a few notes, therefore singers were restricted to those pitches.

By the peak period of the four-part harmony tradition, in the 1700's, the tuning system had evolved to tempered tuning and the bare sound of P5's and P8's was no longer in vogue. Therefore in traditional four-part settings, these consecutive bare sounds are avoided.
*(Contemporary composers sometimes employ these consecutive sounds to achieve special effects.)*

**Play and listen to these chord movements to hear the effect.**

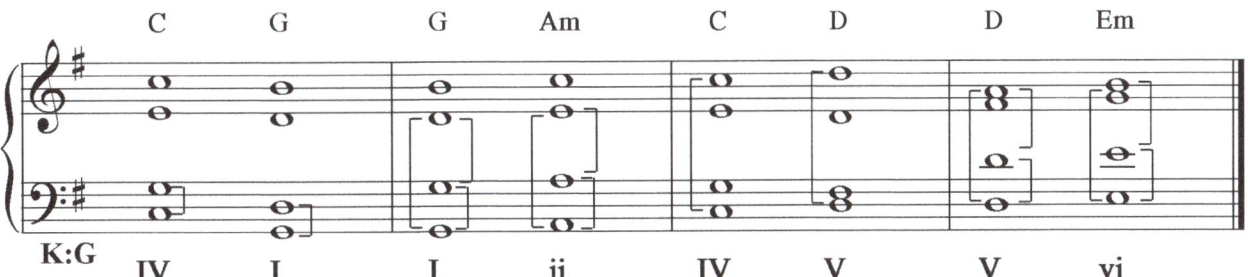

### Special Note

Notes that are repeated in two consecutive chords, remaining at the *same pitch*, are **not** regarded as consecutives. Keep this in mind for later when we will be writing progressions using **first-inversion chords** and **second-inversion chords** in addition to **root-position** chords.

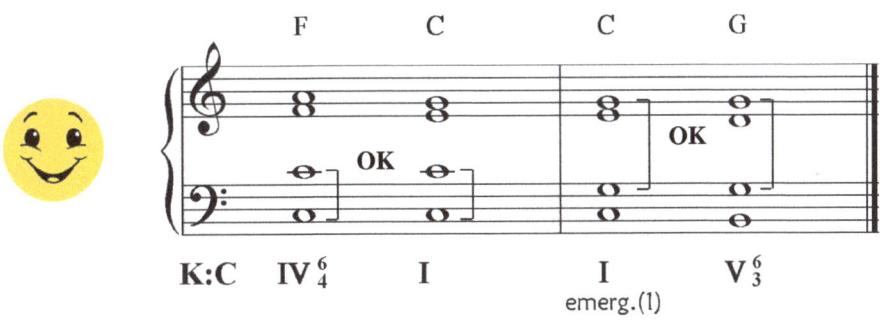

emerg.(1)

# How to Check for Parallel or Consecutive Octaves and Fifths

**SIX CHECKINGS...**
There are six possible combinations of notes which can be written an octave or a fifth apart including the compound versions of the intervals, for instance the Perfect 12th or Compound Perfect 5th and the Perfect 15th or Compound Octave.

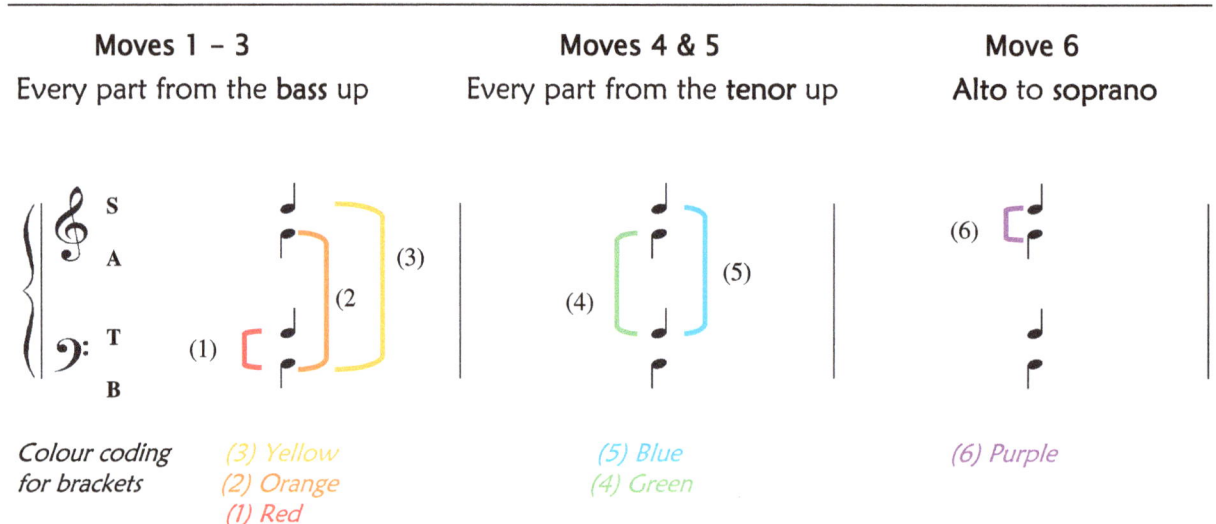

| Moves 1 – 3 | Moves 4 & 5 | Move 6 |
|---|---|---|
| Every part from the **bass** up | Every part from the **tenor** up | **Alto** to **soprano** |

*Colour coding for brackets*
(3) Yellow
(2) Orange
(1) Red

(5) Blue
(4) Green

(6) Purple

*If you find P8's or P5's in two consecutive chords then there is a problem which needs to be corrected. Find the interval and bracket it using the designated colour in both chords, then indicate the problem you have found by writing the number in brackets.*

**For example:**

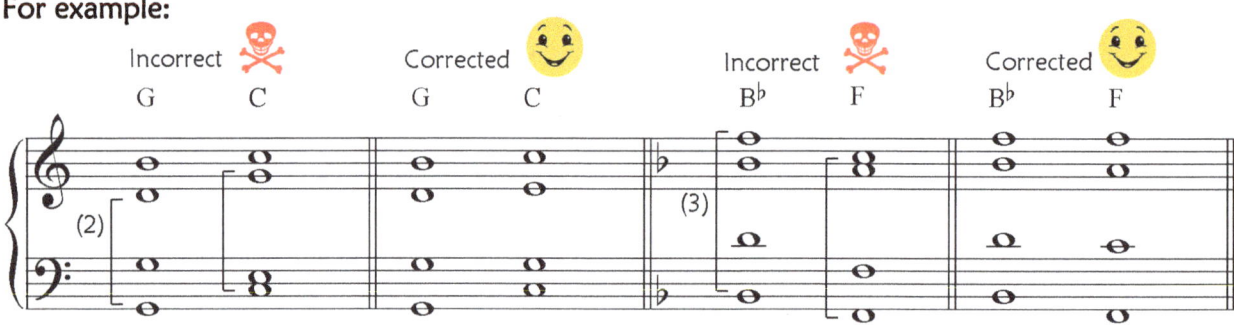

**Harmony Comes Together — STICKY SITUATION — RESCUE CARD**
1) Consecutive P5's can sometimes be corrected by **inverting** them so they become consecutive P4's. Place the notes in different voices to achieve this.
2) Another note of the chord can be inserted so that the consecutive P5 or P8 is avoided. This inserted chord note is known as a **bye-tone**.

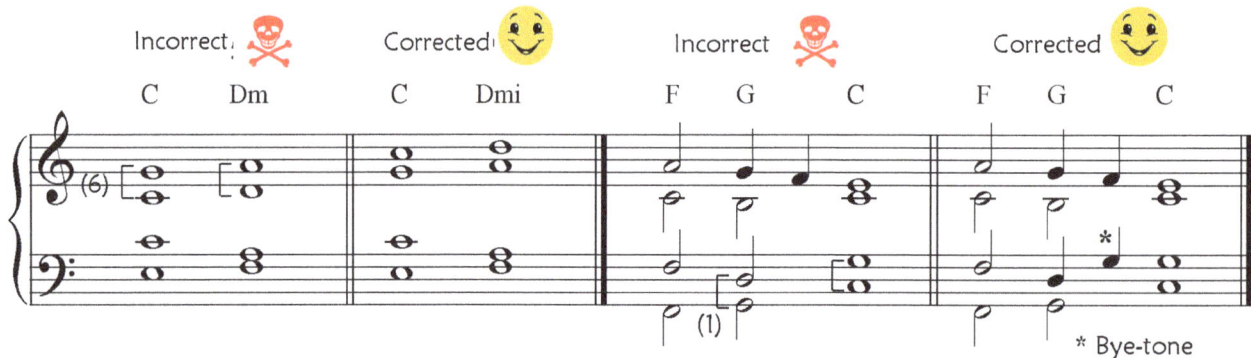

* Bye-tone

# Consecutive P5's & P8's – Search and Rescue

- First write the keys and the chord symbols.
- Then find the **consecutive perfect octaves** and **perfect fifths** in the following progressions.
- Indicate them with a bracket in the appropriate colour.
- Make sure you check all **six** possibilities in each bar.

Refer to the **mind map** on page 28 to see why these consecutives have occurred (*for example: similar motion or wide leaps*) and what to do to avoid them!

## A Special Situation in which Consecutive Fifths are Permitted

Consecutive (parallel) 5ths may be used in the upper three voices,
if one is **diminished** (d5) and the other is **perfect** (P5).

This frequently occurs when chord vii moves to I (VIII).

Example

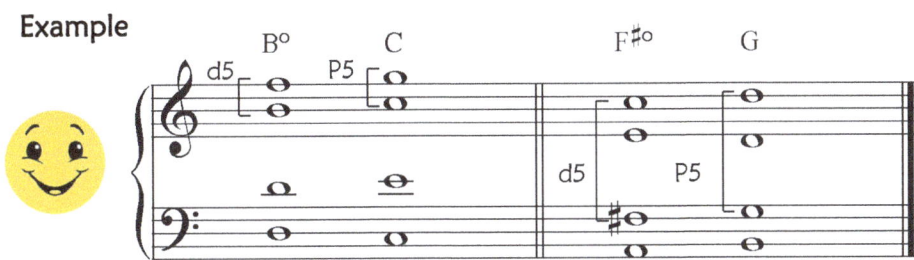

## SOUNDS TO AVOID

## 2) Exposed P5's and P8's

These come about when a set of three occurrences combine:

1) The soprano and bass part move in **similar** motion

2) The **soprano part leaps** (any interval larger than a step)

3) The intervals between the outside notes of the *second* chord are a P8 or a P5

**In other words the progression 'lands' on the P5 or P8 in the second chord, (not in both!)**

**AVOID THESE:**

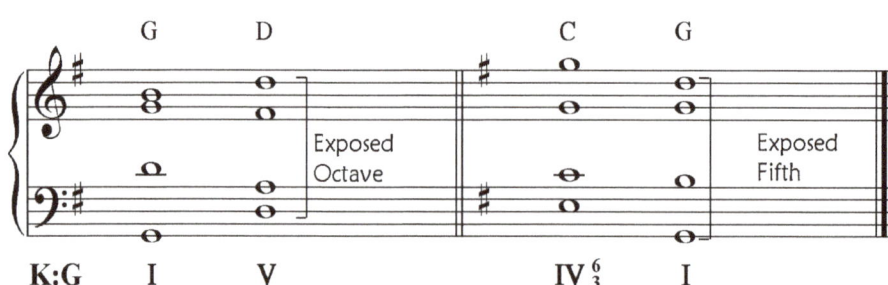

 When are P5's and P8's *not* exposed?

| | OK | | OK |
|---|---|---|---|
| 1) | When the same chord is written in different positions ................................. | | Soprano moves by leap |
| 2) | Between chords **ii** and **V** ............................ | | Soprano goes down a third |
| 3) | At least one chord is **I (i), IV(iv)** or **V**.......... | | Soprano moves by step *(If the soprano is moving by step, there will be no danger in any case.)* |

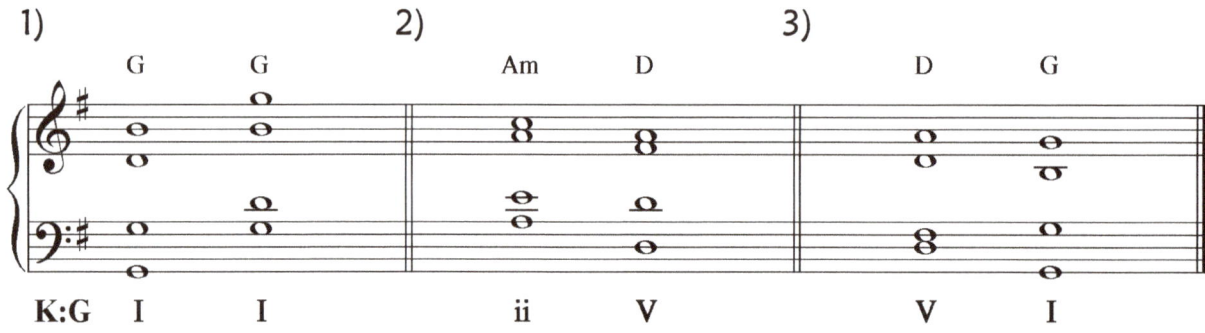

## SOUNDS TO AVOID

## 3) Overlapping of Voices

- Overlapping occurs when one voice is placed higher or lower than the other voice in the following chord. This is generally avoided in four-part writing, although occasionally J.S.Bach creates overlapping parts in Chorale writing to continue the melody for a voice in one direction.

- Overlapping is permitted between two positions of the same chord.

## SOUNDS TO AVOID

## 4) False Relation

- A False Relation occurs when a chromatic note is resolved in another voice.
- Play the example to hear the curious effect.
- The sound can be improved by resolving chromatic notes in the same voice.

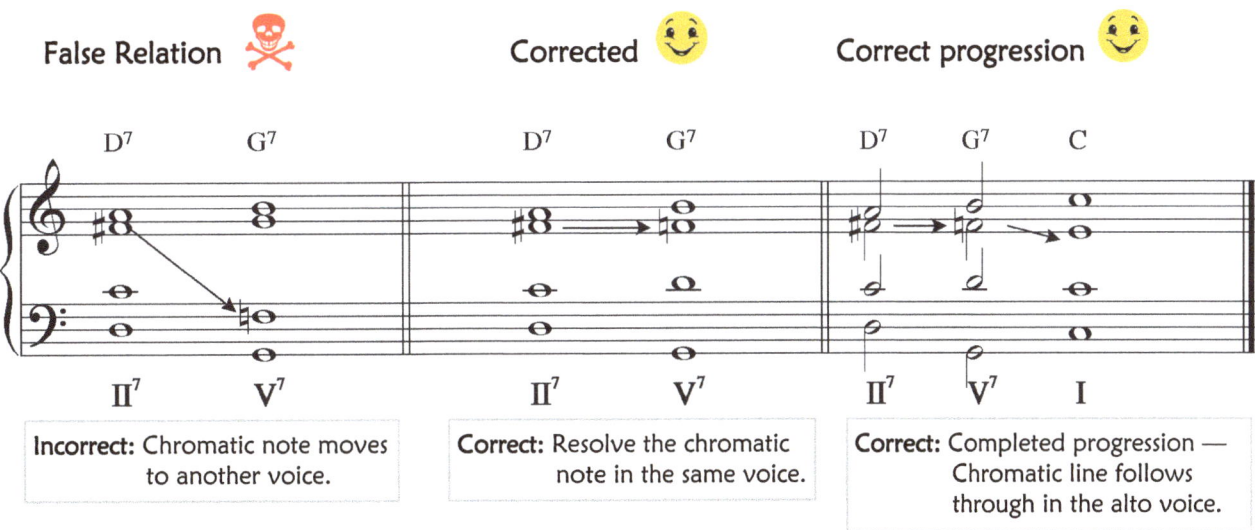

## SOUNDS TO AVOID

### 5) The Intervals of an Augmented 2nd and Augmented 4th in a Melodic Line

- The Augmented 4th (*tritone*) occurs between the 4th and 7th degrees of both the major and harmonic minor scales, as well as in the ascending melodic minor scale.
- The Augmented 2nd occurs between the 6th and 7th degrees of the harmonic minor scale.
- Special care needs to be taken therefore when writing music in a minor key.
- The **melodic minor scale** is less likely to cause problems as it largely avoids these intervals. To avoid augmented 2nd intervals in a melody taken from the harmonic minor scale, approach the **leading note** from above.

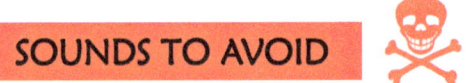

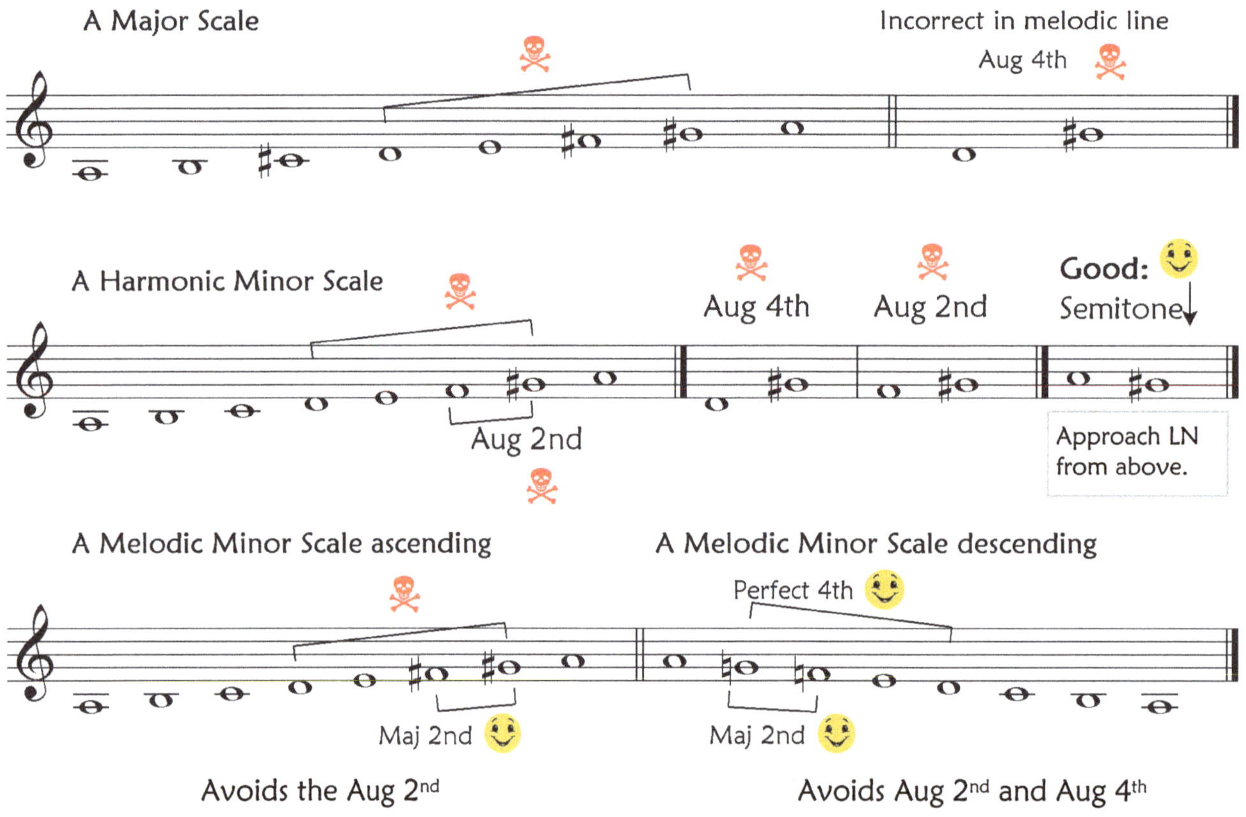


**EXAMPLE**

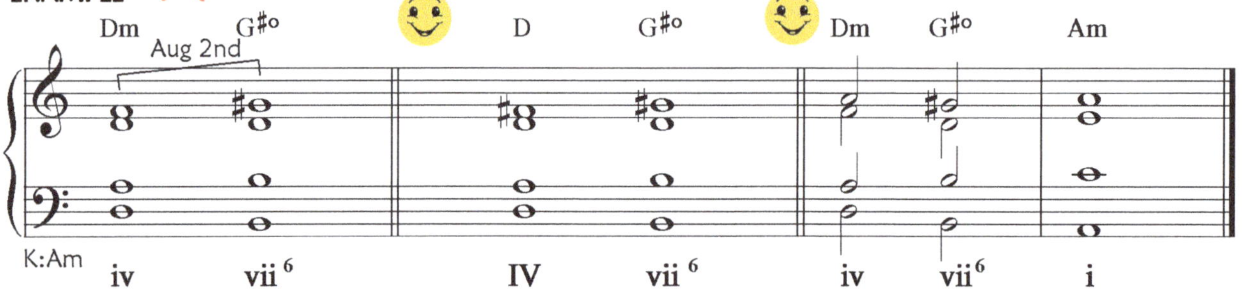


Incorrect: Aug 2nd in soprano

Fix the problem by using notes from the ascending Melodic Minor scale.

Fix the problem by approaching the Leading Note from above.

## SOUNDS TO AVOID

### 6) Doubling the Third Degree in a Major Chord

- In most situations the third degree is not doubled in a **major** chord.
- The doubled major third degree tends to take over as the acoustic root of the chord which affects the stability of the chord and makes it sound somewhat harsh.
- Never double the third of a major chord if it is the *leading note* of the key. (In Chord **V**)

There are a couple of situations when the third degree *may be doubled* in a major chord.

*Colour-code all the doubled thirds on this page - (look for the asterisks )*

1) The doubled third may be used in a **contrary motion** line between the outside parts when it is approached and quitted by **step**. This 'cushions' the sound so that it is quite pleasant. (Occasionally the doubled third may occur in an inner line, if the voice leading demands it.) See the excerpt from Bach Chorale No. 6. for instance of doubled thirds in the outside line.

2) The third is *usually doubled* in Chord **VI** in a progression moving **V** to **VI** in a minor key using both root-position chords to avoid consecutives.
   This progression also forms the **Interrupted Cadence (Deceptive Cadence)**.

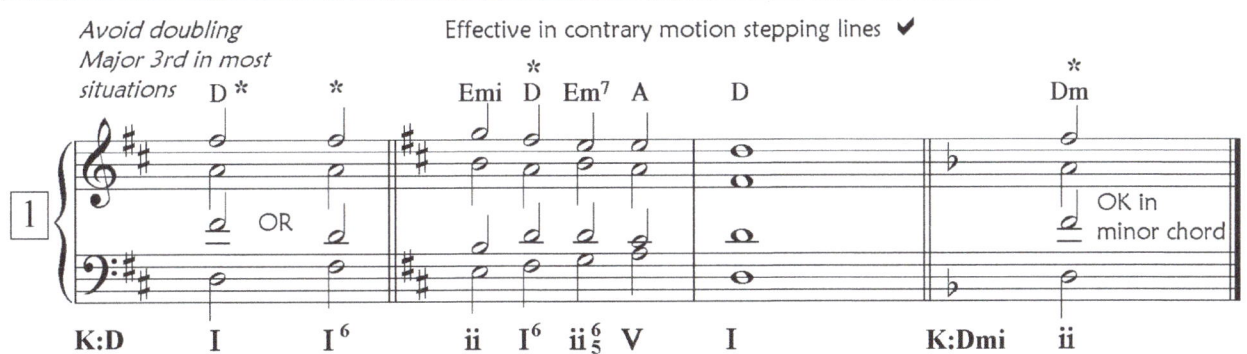

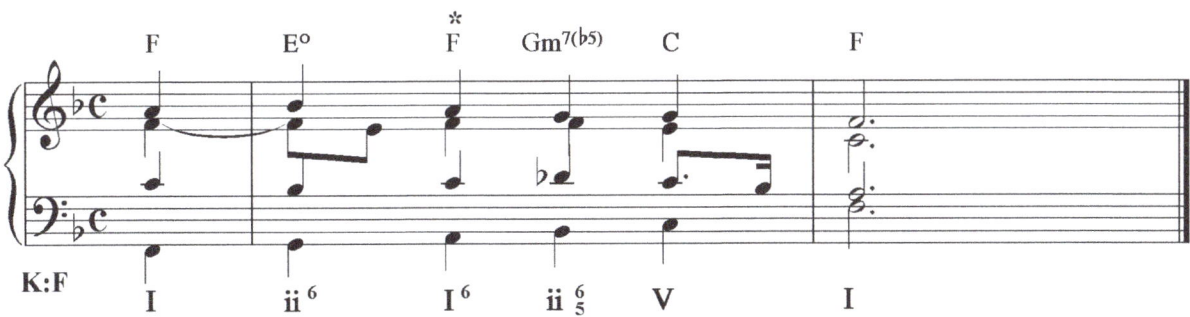

Excerpt: Bach Chorale no. 6 - Christus, der ist mein Leben

Interrupted Cadence

Requires use of doubled 3rd in chord **VI** so that the LN may rise and Consecutive 5ths are avoided

# Root Progressions

- The following progressions should be written, played, listened to and colour-coded.
- Transpose them to several other keys, sounding them at the keyboard.
- Some of the progressions can be used to form cadences. (*See Cadences p74-86)

## Root Progressions – Part One: Primes (Same chords)

**Writing the *same* chord in *different positions* using the 'usual' voicing**
*\* Refer to aims on page 28.*

- In examples (a) (b) and (c) both common notes remain in the same voices.
- Notice the interchange of the 1st and 3rd degrees so that **contrary third movements** are created. This feature is known as *voice exchange.*
- The progressions are effective as they provide variety for one harmony.

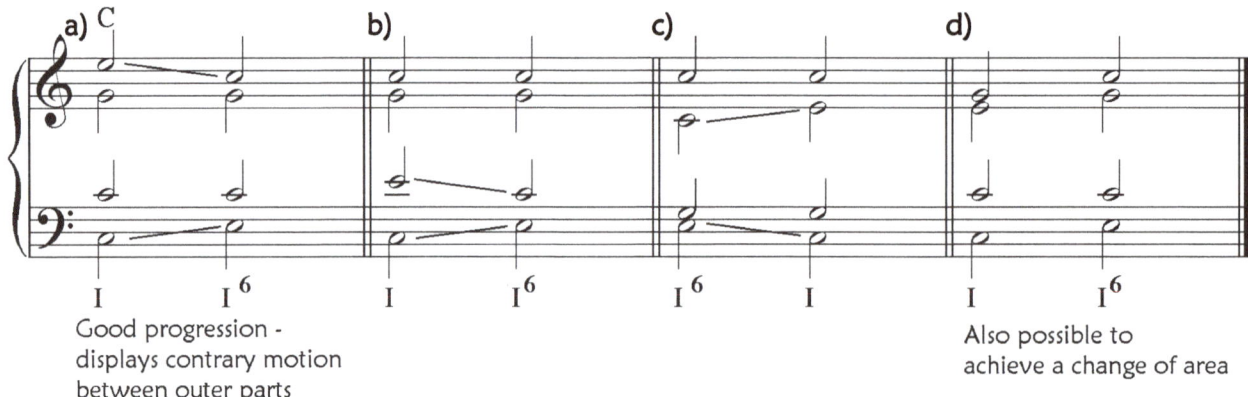

Good progression - displays contrary motion between outer parts

Also possible to achieve a change of area

*Some examples of this progression can be found in the Bach Chorales—Nos 11, 54, 166 & 169.*

'Writing Recipe' for types a), b) and c)

- Write a correct setting for the first chord.
- Write the notes of each voice in the **second** chord of the progression in *writing recipe* order.
- Work from the bass note up.

| 4 | Left-over part |
| 3 | CN |
| 2 | Common note (CN) |
| 1 | Bass note (BN) |

The progression of chords from root position to first inversion provides an ideal situation for the insertion of passing notes for decoration.

*\* More examples of passing notes can be found on page 92.*
*\* An extended section on decorative notes appears in book two of this series.*

# Procedure for Completing the Questions on the Following Pages

1) Write a chord table for the key in the box provided, or draw boxes for tables on paper
2) Work out the name of each chord and write the chord symbols above the treble staff
3) Write the chords in four parts and colour-code the doubled notes.

## Question One

- Write these progressions in a **major key** using the **'usual'** voicing for all major and minor chords.
- Use the required doubling for any diminished chords.
- Keep the **common notes** in the same parts where possible.
- Indicate any **contrary motion** between the parts with coloured lines.

**Table for G Major**

K: G  I  $I^6$  *  $I^6$  I   ii  $ii^6$  $ii^6$  ii   IV  $IV^6$  $IV^6$  IV

V  $V^6$  $V^6$  V   vi  $vi^6$  $vi^6$  vi   $vii^6$  $vii^6$  $vii^6$  $vii^6$

\* Write the first bar, then simply reverse the chords for the second bar.

Usual  Emerg.1  Emerg.1  Usual
(for dim)

## Question Two

- Write these progressions in a **minor key** working in the same manner as for question one.

**Table for D Minor**

K: Dmi  i  $i^6$  $i^6$  i   iv  $iv^6$  $iv^6$  iv

V  $V^6$  $V^6$  V   VI  $VI^6$  $VI^6$  VI   $vii^6$  $vii^6$  $vii^6$  $vii^6$

Usual  Emerg.1  Emerg.1  Usual

# Root Progressions – Part Two

## Root Movement by Thirds and Sixths

- Any progression where the **root movement** is by **thirds** or **sixths** has a fairly weak sound owing to the larger amount of common notes between the chords.
- The weakest progression is where the root movement is *up* by a third.
- These progressions are therefore often used to provide a change of aural colour within the bar, particularly from a strong to a weak beat.

---

**Available chords:** all chords in **first inversion** and all chords in **root position** except diminished chords and the augmented chord.

Major Key      I   ii   iii   IV   V   vi   vii°   VIII   ii

Minor Key      i   ii°   III   iv   V   VI   vii°   viii   ii°

The progressions **iii -V** and **iii⁶ - V** are extremely weak and therefore rarely used.

## Part Two A: Third Up (↑3) – Sixth Down (↓6)

**Study the following progressions and relate them to the line diagram.**
1) How many common notes occur when the two chords appear in root position? ..........
2) Which way does the other upper part move? ......................................
3) Did you notice that the bass can move either up or down? .................

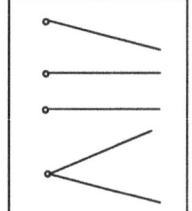

*The upper three part movements can be placed in any voice.*

This is the standard look of the progression
when both chords are in root position.
Other variations may occur when inversions are used.

### 'Writing Recipe' for the Second Chord When Both Chords are in Root Position

| | |
|---|---|
| 4 | Left-over part |
| 3 | CN |
| 2 | CN |
| 1 | BN |

**Emergency 1 —** used to introduce contrary motion between tenor and alto voices.

**EXAMPLES**

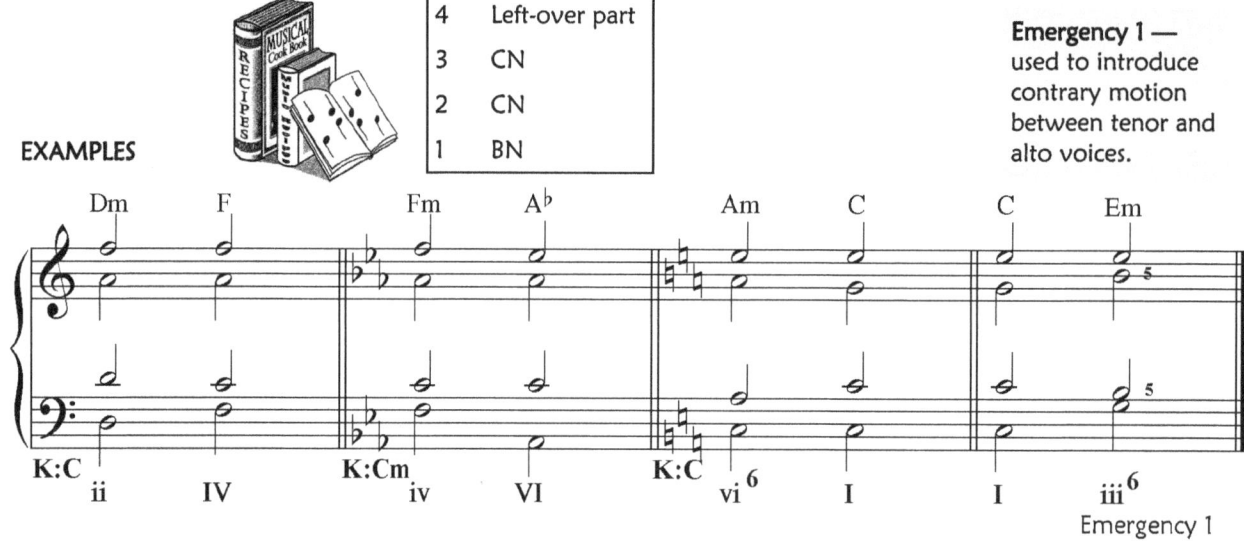

Emergency 1

# Questions: Part Two A (↑3) – (↓6) in Root Position

- Follow the 'Writing Recipe' on the previous page to write these progressions.
- Track their movements with a different coloured arrows on the Chord Table.
- You should find that several progressions move to chords that lie above and below one another in the table.

|  |  |  |
|---|---|---|
| IV | I | V |
| ii | vi | iii |
|  |  | vii° |

(IV ← ii indicated by arrow)

## Question One
- Write these progressions in a major key.
- Keep the **common notes** in the same parts where possible.
- Complete a chord table and write the chord symbols above the treble staff as before.
- Finish by colour-coding the doubled notes.

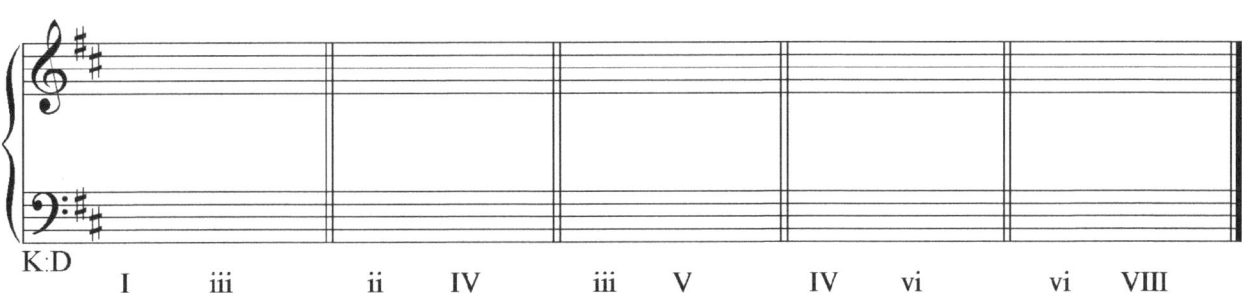

K:D    I   iii    ii   IV    iii   V    IV   vi    vi   VIII

## Question Two
- Write these progressions in a minor key.
- Follow the same plan as for Question One.

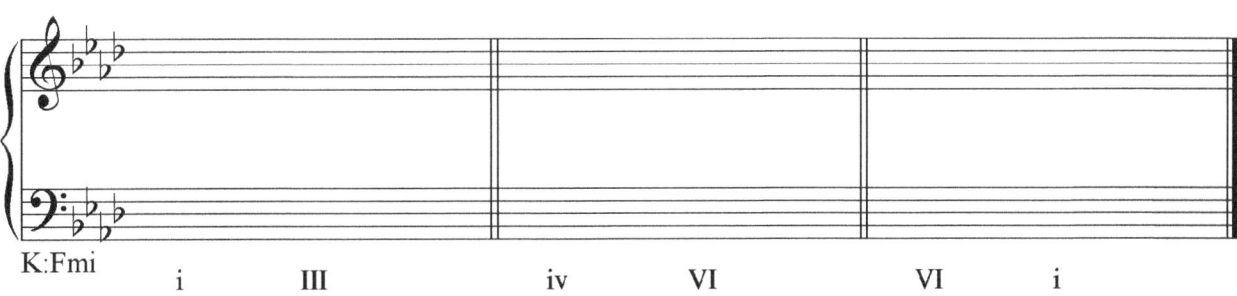

K:Fmi    i   III    iv   VI    VI   i

> From this point on, always write the chord symbols above the treble staff before completing the four-part notation of the chords.

# Questions: Part Two A (↑3) - (↓6)
## Mixing Root-Position & First-Inversion Chords

- Aim for the 'usual' voicing for each chord. However if a large leap occurs, experiment with Emergency 1 (2x5ths) in either the first or the second chord, in order to *smooth out the voicing* or to *introduce contrary motion* between the parts.
- Remember that the standard look for these progressions, (see p38) does *not* apply when there is a mixture of root-position and first-inversion chords.

> *Curious Facts No.1*
> When writing a smooth progression using a mix of **root-position** and **first-inversion** chords, it often works out, that the degree of the chord assigned to the soprano part, is the one that requires doubling in the first-inversion chord.

### Question One

- Write these progressions in a major key.
- Keep the **common notes** in the same parts where possible.
- *Remember to double the third or the fifth in a diminished chord.*

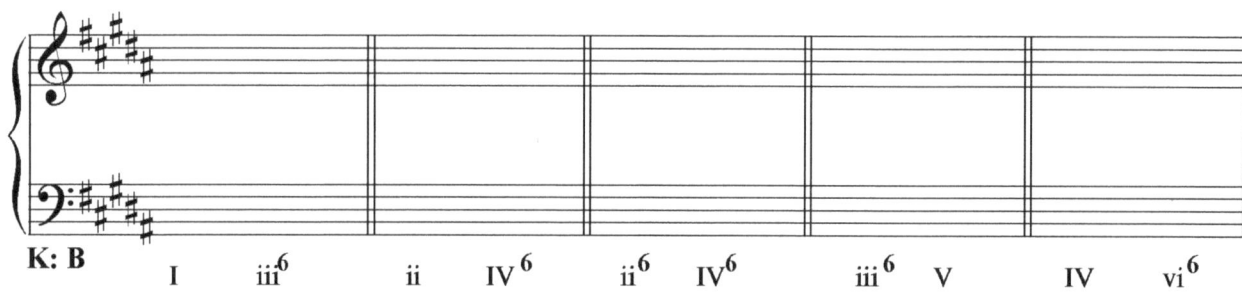

K: B    I   iii$^6$    ii   IV$^6$    ii$^6$   IV$^6$    iii$^6$   V    IV   vi$^6$

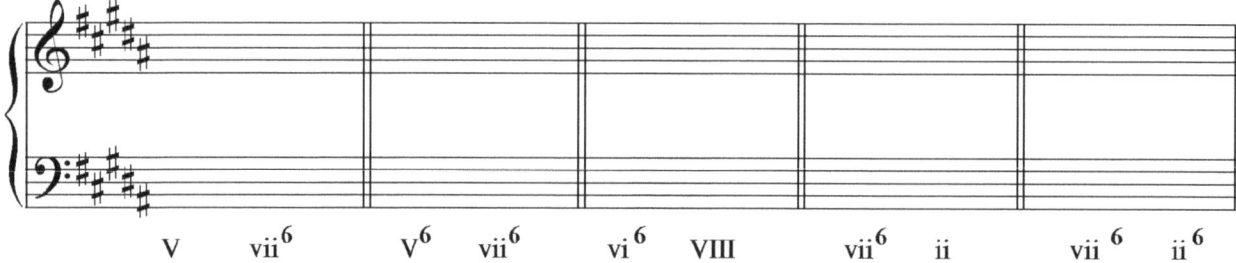

V   vii$^6$    V$^6$   vii$^6$    vi$^6$   VIII    vii$^6$   ii    vii$^6$   ii$^6$

### Question Two

- Write these progressions in a **minor** key.
- Work in the same manner as before.

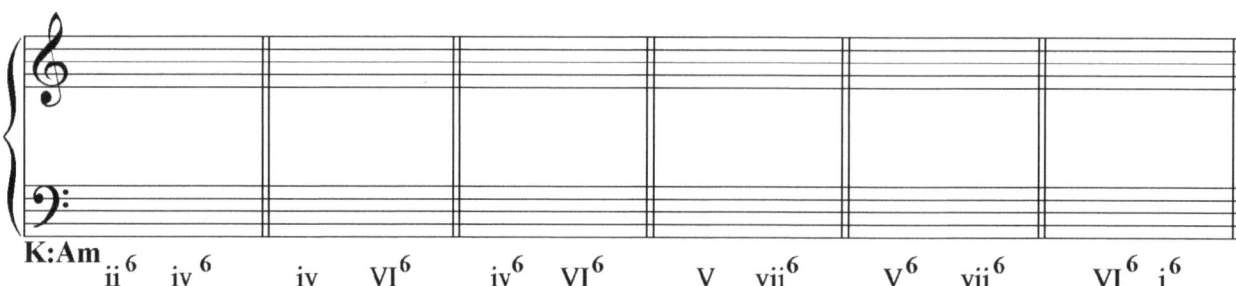

K:Am   ii$^6$   iv$^6$    iv   VI$^6$    iv$^6$   VI$^6$    V   vii$^6$    V$^6$   vii$^6$    VI$^6$   i$^6$

# Root Progressions — Part Two B: Third Down (↓3) - Sixth Up (↑6)

Root Progressions in which the bass moves down a third, (↓3) are regarded as one of the primary progressions. They have more sense of movement than those progressions which move up by a third, as the bass note of the second chord has not already been sounded as one of the notes of the first chord. Therefore these progressions have stronger harmonic effect than the progressions in Part Two A.

## Study the following progressions and relate them to the line diagram.

1) How many common notes occur when the two chords appear in root position? ............
2) Which way does the other upper part move? ..................................
3) Did you notice that the bass can move either up or down? ..................

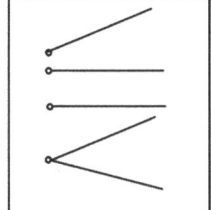

*The upper three part movements can be placed in any voice.*

This is the standard look of the progression
when both chords are in root position.
Other variations may occur when inversions are used.

### EXAMPLES

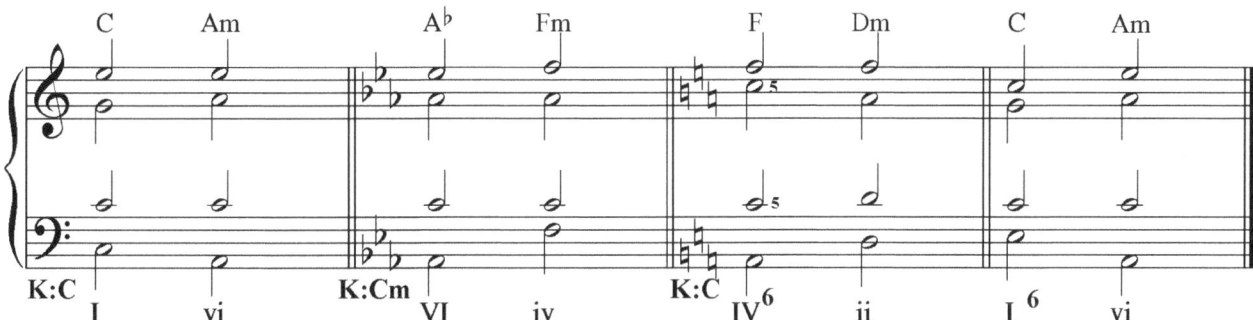

*Progressions* **iii — I** *and* **V — iii** *are quite weak and therefore rarely used.*

### Root-Position Progressions Moving by Falling Thirds or Rising Sixths

**Question One**
- Write these progressions in a major key.
- Keep the **common notes** in the same parts where possible.
- Track the chord movements on the Chord Table using arrows.

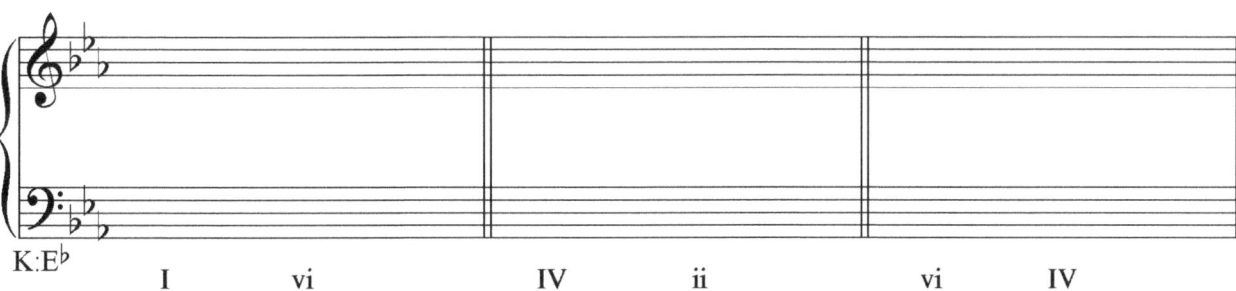

# Questions: Part Two B (↓3) – (↑6)

### Question Two
- Write these progressions in **minor** keys.
- Draw chord tables on a separate sheet of paper and track the movements.

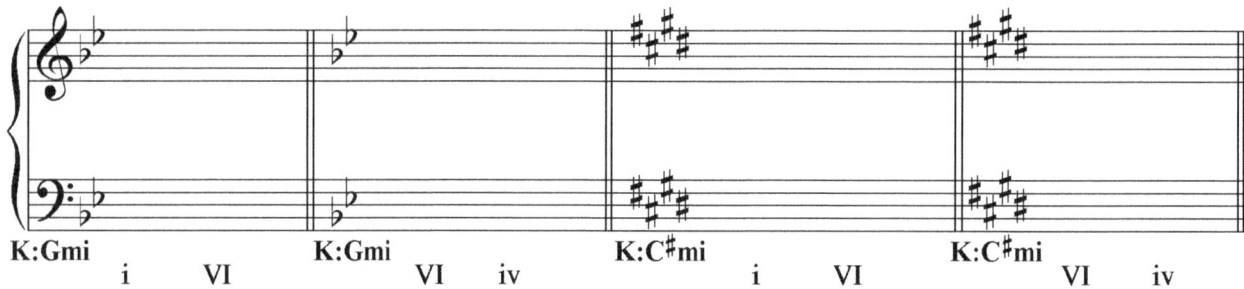

K:Gmi    i    VI      K:Gmi    VI    iv      K:C♯mi    i    VI      K:C♯mi    VI    iv

---

**Mixing Root-Position and First-Inversion Chords**

- Aim for the usual voicing for each chord.
- However if a large leap occurs, experiment with **Emergency 1** voicing, (2x5ths), in either the first or the second chord in order to smooth out the line or to introduce contrary motion between the parts.

---

### Question Three
- Write these progressions in a major key.
- *Remember to double the third or the fifth in a diminished chord.*

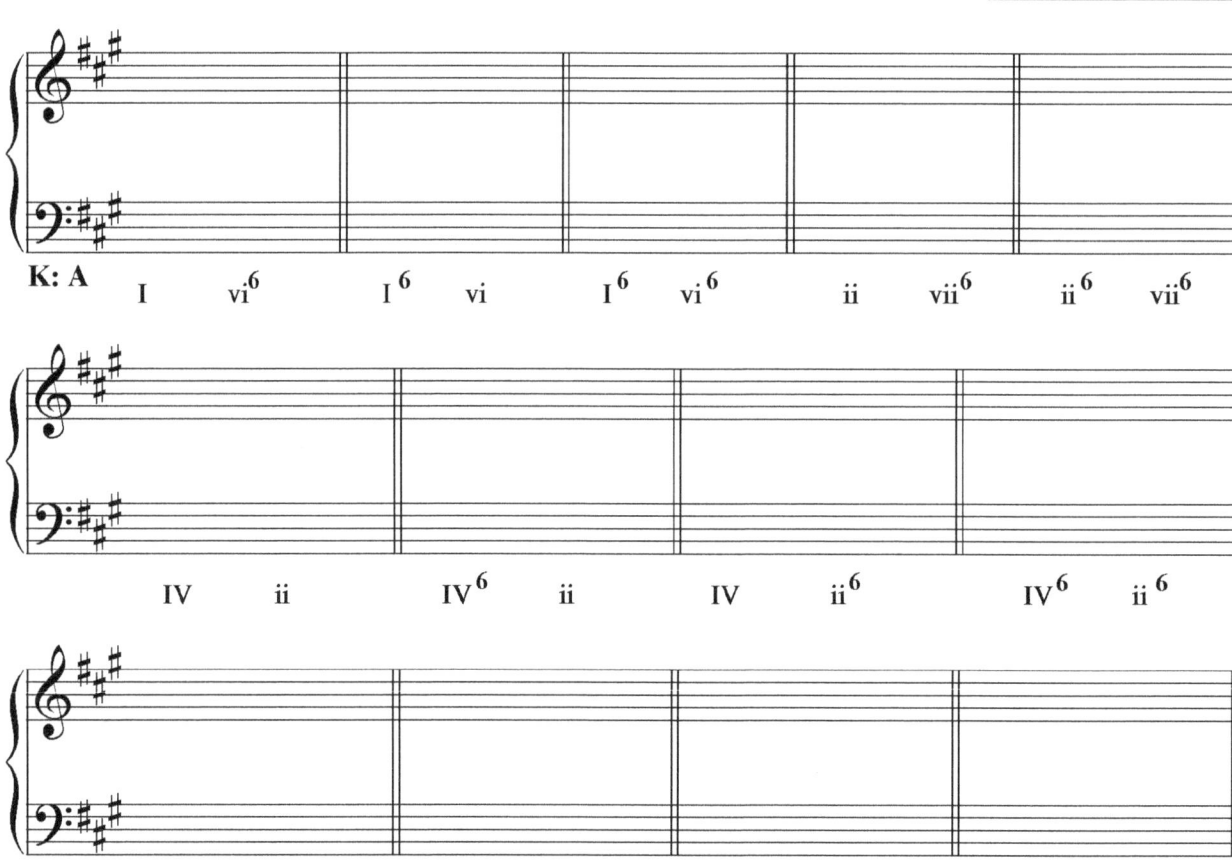

K: A    I    vi$^6$    I$^6$    vi    I$^6$    vi$^6$    ii    vii$^6$    ii$^6$    vii$^6$

IV    ii    IV$^6$    ii    IV    ii$^6$    IV$^6$    ii$^6$

vi    IV    vi$^6$    IV    vi    IV$^6$    vi$^6$    IV$^6$

# More Questions: Part Two B (↓3) – (↑6)

### Question Four
- Write these progressions in both the major and the minor key — then compare them.

*The diminished chord on **vii** can provide slight variations to the dominant harmony. It can therefore be used to spin out the dominant harmony if it is required for a longer time.*

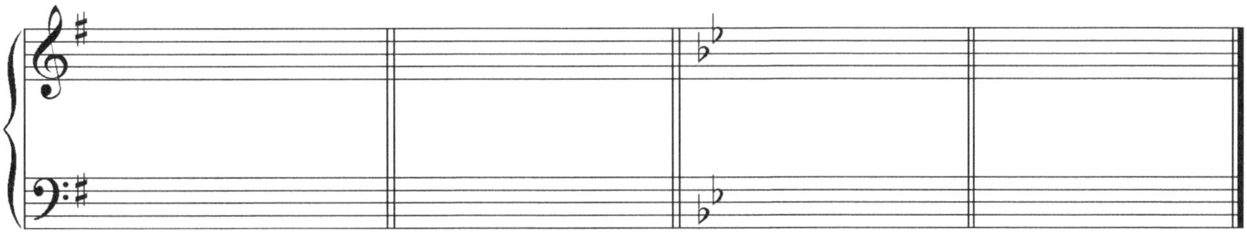

K:G    vii⁶   V    vii⁶   V⁶    K:Gmi    vii⁶   V    vii⁶   V⁶

? *Did you notice the common notes between the two chords in each of the above progressions? Owing to the number of common notes and the fact that both chords include the LN of the key, the two chords are often used to **substitute** for one another in a progression that continues on to chords **I(i)** or **vi (VI)**.*

---

**Harmony Comes Together — STICKY SITUATION — RESCUE CARD**

Avoid augmented seconds in a melodic line — approach the leading note from above!

---

### Question Five
- Write these progressions in a **minor** key.

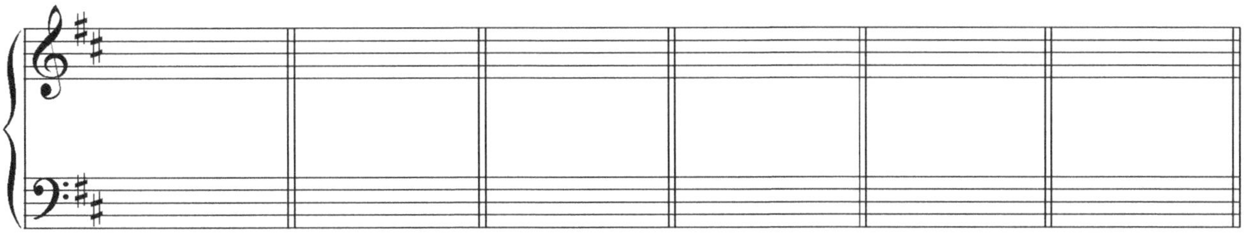

K: Bmi   i  VI   i  VI⁶   i⁶  VI   i⁶  VI⁶   iv  ii⁶   iv⁶  ii⁶

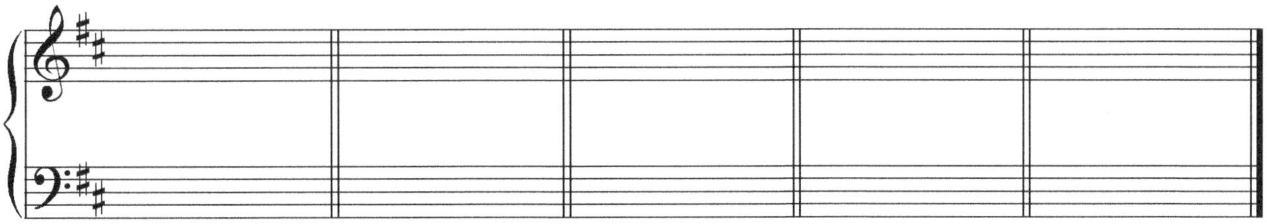

VI  iv   VI⁶  iv   VI  iv⁶   VI⁶  iv⁶   ii⁶  vii⁶

# Root Progressions – Part Three

## Root Movement by Fourths and Fifths

- **Root movement** by *rising* fourths (↑4) or *falling* fifths (↓5) produces a very solid and satisfying sound of pleasing resolution. The root movement is anti-clockwise around the Cycle of Fifths.

- **Root movement** by *falling* fourths (↓4) or *rising* fifths (↑5) is a weaker movement and if used in a series creates tension. The root movement is clockwise around the Cycle of Fifths.

**Available chords:** all chords in **first inversion** and all chords in **root position** except diminished chords.

## Part Three A:   Fourth Up (↑4) — Fifth Down (↓5)

Study the following progressions and relate them to the line diagram.

### THE USUAL LOOK

1) How many common notes occur when the two chords appear in root position? ..............
2) Which way do the other upper parts move? ...................
3) Did you notice that the bass can move either up or down? .....................

*The upper three part movements can be placed in any voice.*

This is the standard look of the progression
when both chords are in root position.
Other variations may occur when inversions are used.

The **root movement** is anti-clockwise around the Cycle of Fifths.

### EXAMPLES

In a **V-I** (**V-i**) progression the 7th degree leads to the tonic (1st or 8th).

In a **I-IV** (**i-iv**) progression the 3rd degree leads to the 4th degree.

The **V-I** (**V-i**) progression can be used as an ending formula known as a **Perfect Cadence**.
(**Authentic Cadence**)   *See pages 74 to 77*

# Questions: Part Three A (↑4) - (↓5) in Root Position

'Writing Recipe' for the Second Chord When Both Chords are in Root Position

```
4    ↗
3    ↗
2    CN
1    BN
```

## Question One
- Write these progressions in a major key.
- Keep the **common notes** in the same part.
- Write the bass part going either way, depending on the arrow.
- Track the chord movements on the Chord Table.

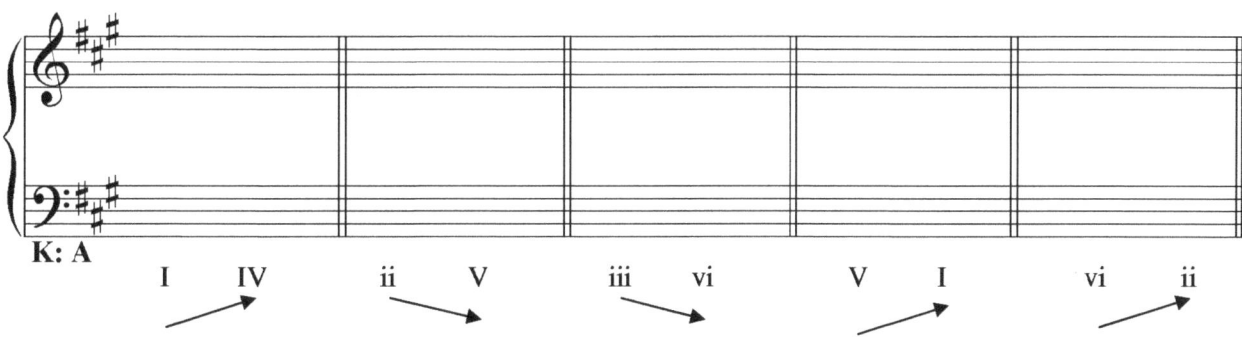

## Question Two
- Write these progressions in a **minor** key.
- Track the chord movements on the Chord Table.
- What do you notice about the direction in which the progressions travel? ..................................................................................

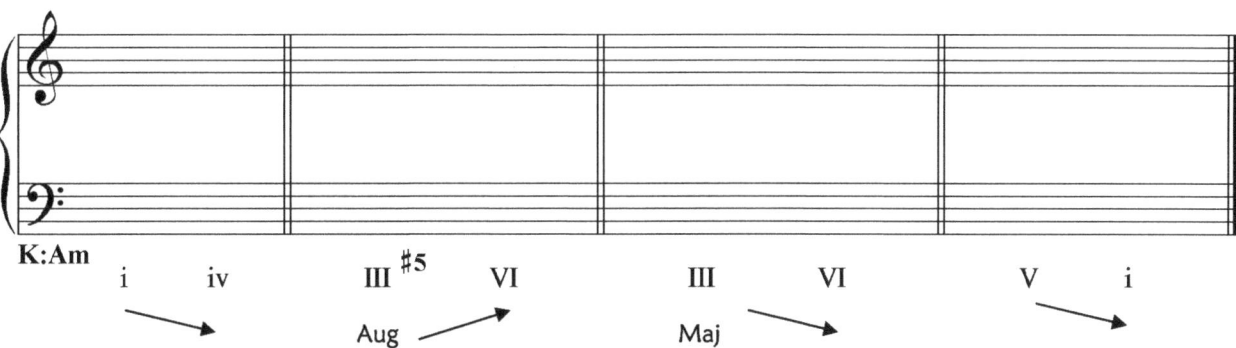

## PART THREE A¹ — Falling-Fifth Progressions with *Falling* Soprano Melody Lines

In these progressions the part movements are **not the usual** movements seen on page 45. The second chord may employ an emergency voicing, or variations to the standard part movements may occur. *Colour-code all the examples on this page to discover the settings.*

### Special Ways to Treat the V–I (V–i) Progression when the Melody Falls: 2–1

'Writing Recipe' for Example A
- Both chords are in **root position** using Emergency 2 voicing in the second chord.

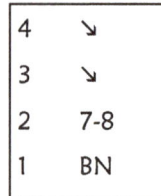

A & B —these settings are often used as part of the 3-2-1 (Three Blind Mice) ending, using the **V-I (V-i)** progression.

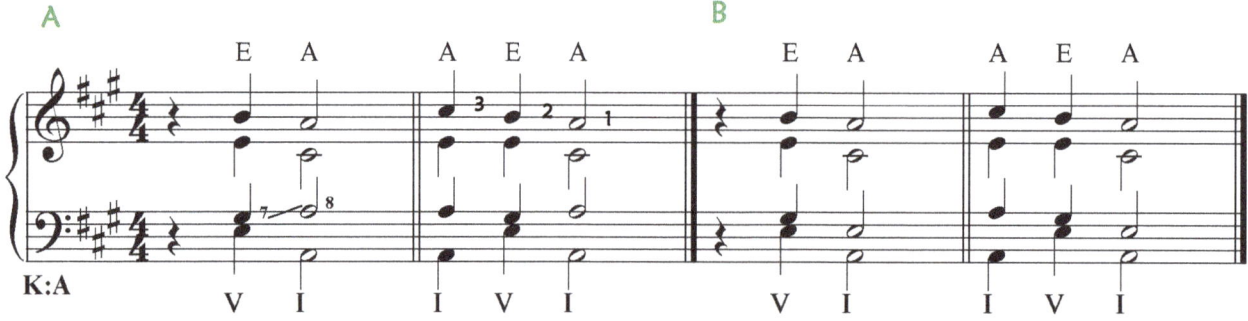

**A** The 7-8 move takes precedence over the common note. Colour-code both chords to see how this works.

**B** This is known as the **Bach Cadence.** Here the leading note does not rise, which is OK as it is in an inner part. The result is a fuller sound for the final chord as it is a 'usual' setting.

---

### Question One
- On separate manuscript, write progressions A and B in the keys of E♭ major and D minor.

## MORE SPECIAL TREATMENTS

**C** — Special treatment for the **V– I (V– i )** progression when the melody falls using degrees 5-3

**D & E** — Examples of falling melody lines in the I—IV (I –iv) and ii –V progressions
**F** — The ii –V progression resolved to the tonic triad

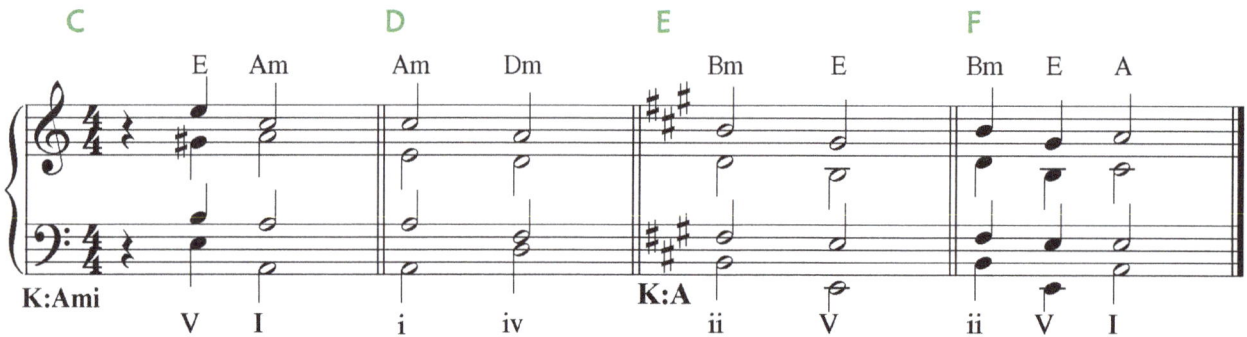

Common note is sacrificed. Leading note is resolved to the tonic.

Soprano and Bass in contrary motion to avoid an exposed 5th.

A common treatment of the **ii -V** progression where the melody falls by a third.

# More Questions: Part Three A (↑4) - (↓5)

## Question Two
- Complete the remaining three voices in these progressions which use descending soprano melody lines. Colour-code to check all your settings on this page.

K: F    I   IV   ii   V   iii   vi   V   I   vi   ii

## Question Three
- Write these progressions using descending soprano melody lines.

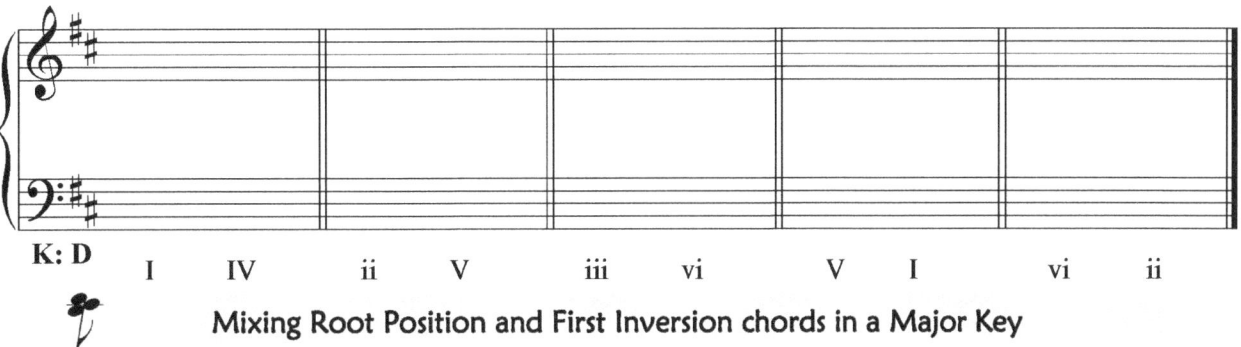

K: D    I   IV   ii   V   iii   vi   V   I   vi   ii

### Mixing Root Position and First Inversion chords in a Major Key

## Question Four
- Use the 'usual' voicing or 'emergency 1' (2x 5ths) to smooth out any bumps!

K: B♭   $I^6$   IV   I   $IV^6$   $I^6$   $IV^6$   $ii^6$   V   ii   $V^6$

$iii^6$   $vi^6$   IV   $vii^6$   $IV^6$   $vii^6$   V   $I^6$   $V^6$   I   $V^6$   $I^6$

vi   $ii^6$   $vi^6$   ii   $vi^6$   $ii^6$   $vii^6$   iii

## More Questions: Part Three A (↑4) - (↓5) and Extended Progressions

**Question Five**
- Indicate the chord symbols then write these progressions in minor key.
- Take care to avoid augmented 2nds and 4ths in any melodic line.

> Move upper three parts contrary to the bass

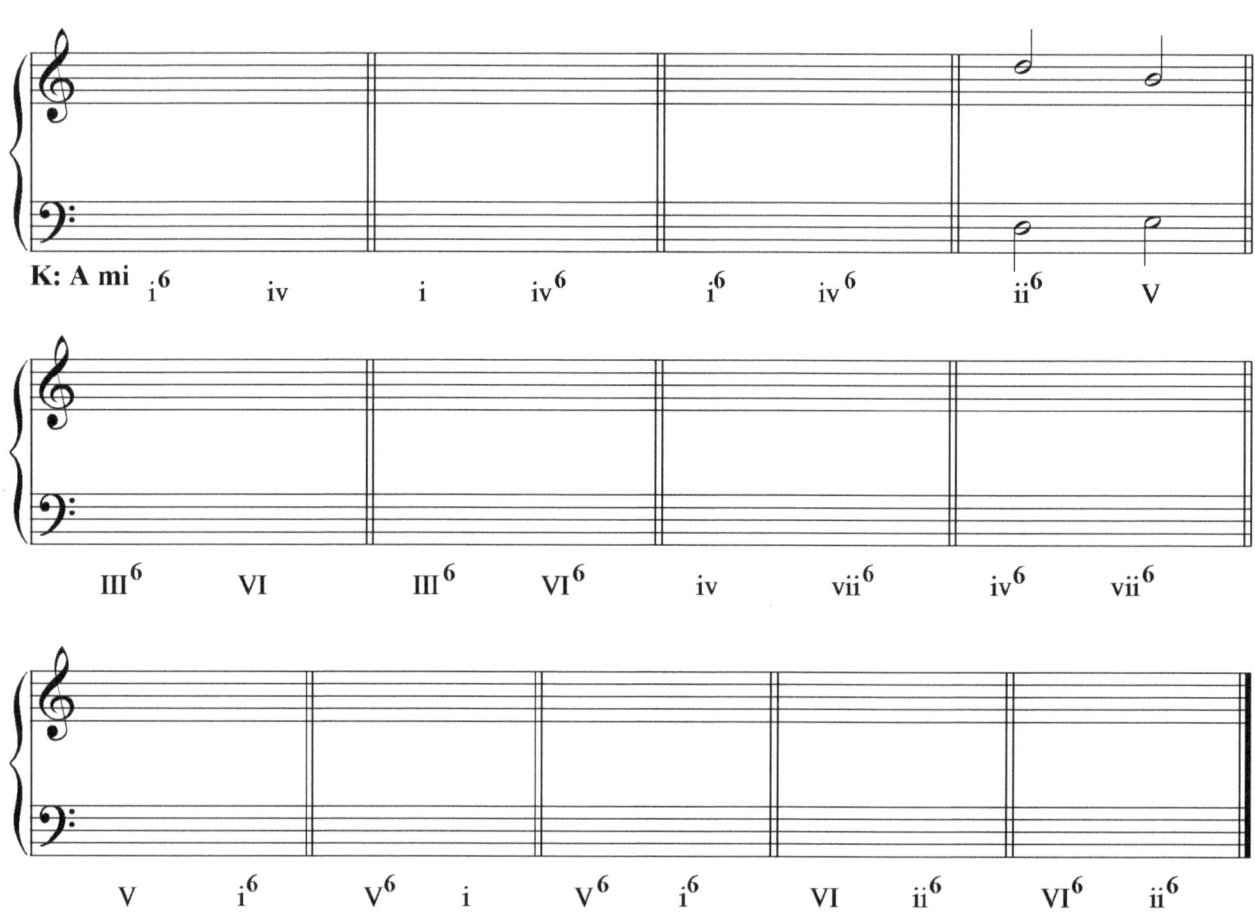

K: A mi  i⁶  iv  i  iv⁶  i⁶  iv⁶  ii⁶  V

III⁶  VI  III⁶  VI⁶  iv  vii⁶  iv⁶  vii⁶

V  i⁶  V⁶  i  V⁶  i⁶  VI  ii⁶  VI⁶  ii⁶

---

**Harmony Comes Together—Extended progressions using Root Progressions 1, 2A, 2B and 3A**
- Write the inner voices of these progressions. Indicate the RP's below the staves.

K:C  I  I⁶  IV  IV⁶  ii  ii⁶  V  V⁶  I     K:Ami  i  III⁺⁵  VI  ii⁶  V♯  V⁶  i

K:C  I  vi  IV  ii  V⁶  V  I     K:Ami  i  iv⁶  iv  ii⁶  V♯  V♯  i

# Sequences using Rising Fourths/Falling Fifths

A sequence is created when the same melodic pattern is repeated at a higher or lower pitch.

For instance:

- As we have already discovered, **root movement** by *rising* fourths / *falling* fifths produces a very solid and satisfying sound of pleasing resolution.
- A frequently used harmonic sequence, is the progression in which the root movement moves **anti-clockwise** around the Cycle of Fifths.

**If the progression remains in one major key, the degree numbers are as follows:**

I   IV   vii   iii   vi   ii   V   I

| Here is the movement of the progression around the Cycle of Fifths in the key of B Flat. |
|---|

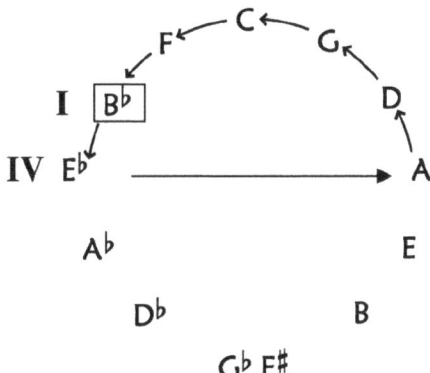

| Write the remainder of the chord degree numbers next to the letter names on the cycle. |
|---|

Special Note:   If a **diminished** chord occurs in a sequence then it may be used in root position and the root may be doubled! (Here is your chance to break rules!)

This progression is a favourite in many Baroque and Classical compositions and occurs frequently in Jazz and popular tunes, either in its entirety or in smaller sections.

Classical:   J.S Bach's *Invention XIII in A minor* and Mozart's *Sonata in Ami K310*
Jazz:        *Bluesette* by Jazz composer Toots Thielmans
Popular:     *I Will Survive* and *Fantasy* (both disco tunes),
             *You're a Lady* by pop composer Peter Skellern, *Wild World* by Cat Stevens

| Find some more examples of *Cycle of Fifth* progressions in the music you are playing and studying. List them here: _____ |
|---|
| _____ |
| _____ |
| _____ |

# 'Cycle of Fifths' Progressions

## Example One — Using Root-Position Chords

Note the use of the beginning chord as an **anacrusis.** This sets up the harmonic rhythm — the frequency of use of each chord within a bar. Emphasis is placed on the **rest chords** which occur on the strong beats, while the **leading-function chords** occur on the weaker beats. *The upper three parts may be swapped around.*

**Exercises:**
1) Continue writing the degree numbers of the upper three parts so you can discover the movement of the parts.
2) Write a Chord Table for the key and track the chord progression using coloured arrows.

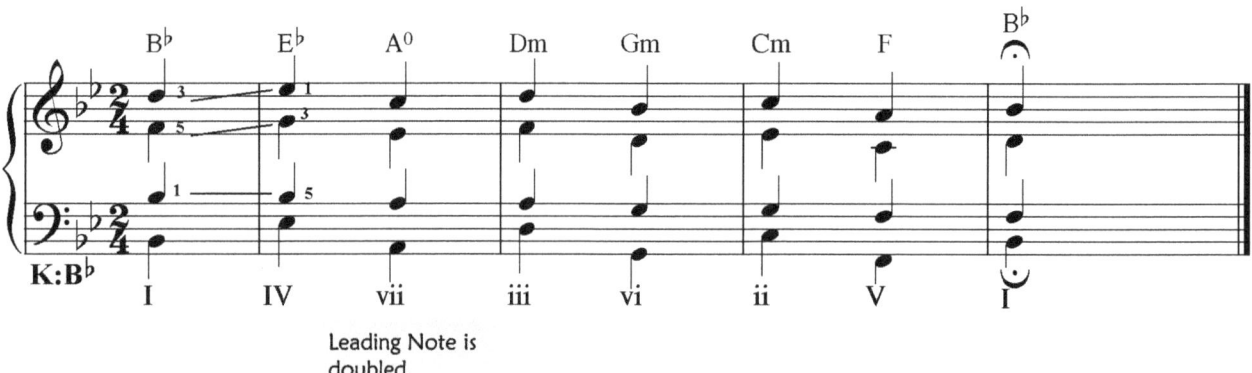

Leading Note is doubled.

## Example Two — Using Alternating Root-Position and First-Inversion Chords

**Exercise:** Continue writing the degree numbers of the upper three parts to discover the movement of the parts.

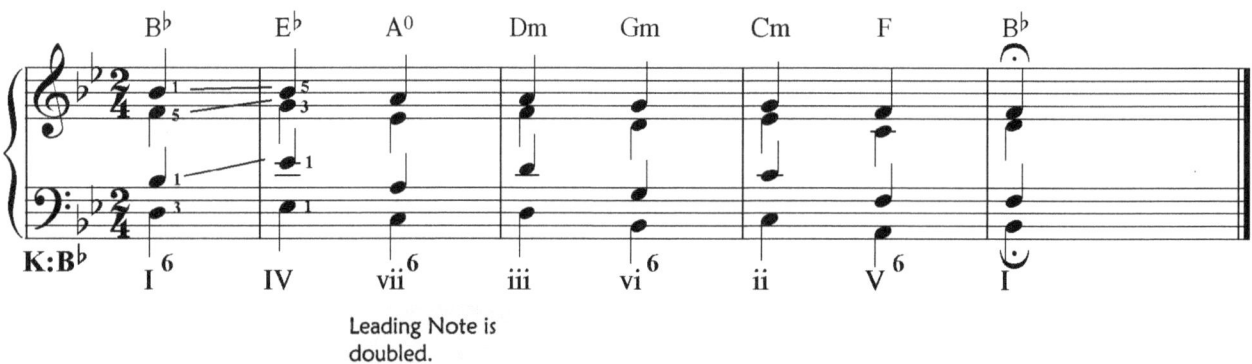

Leading Note is doubled.

## Modern Keyboard Skill

Play both of the above progressions in **piano style**, using the following rhythms ...

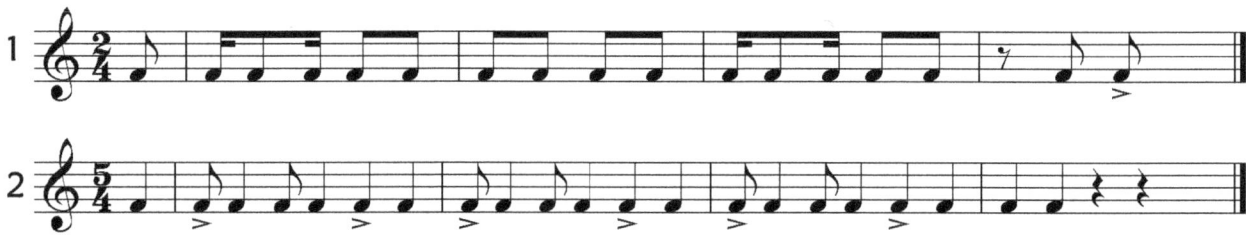

# Transposition – 'Cycle of Fifths' Progressions

**Preparation for questions one and two**
- Write a chord table for the key of D major.
- Write the chord symbols for each example.

1) Transpose example one from the previous page to the key of D major.
   Write this progression in *four-part vocal* style.

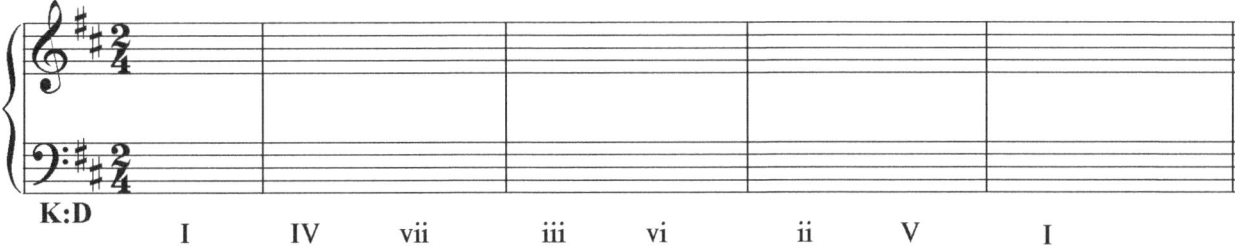

K:D    I    IV    vii    iii    vi    ii    V    I

2) Transpose example two from the previous page to the key of D major.
   Write this progression in *piano* style.

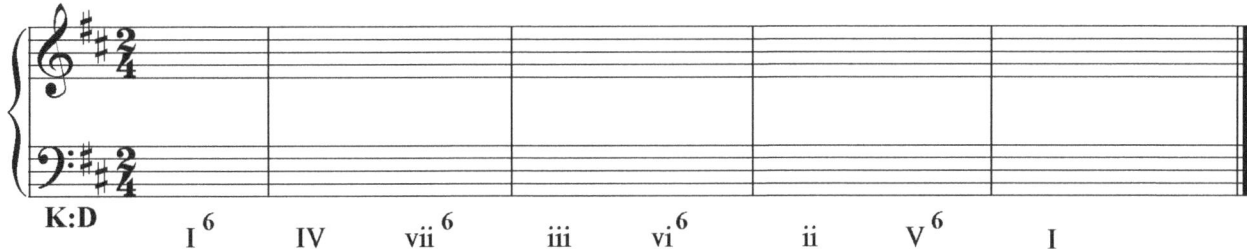

K:D    I$^6$    IV    vii$^6$    iii    vi$^6$    ii    V$^6$    I

---

**EXAMPLES a) and b)**

**Cycle of Fifth Progression in a Minor key** —This progression makes use of the **VII** (Subtonic) from the descending melodic minor scale (or natural minor) scale. This allows the progression to continue without needing to resolve, until the final two chords — Dominant to Tonic.

---

3) On separate manuscript, transpose examples a) and b) to the key of A minor.

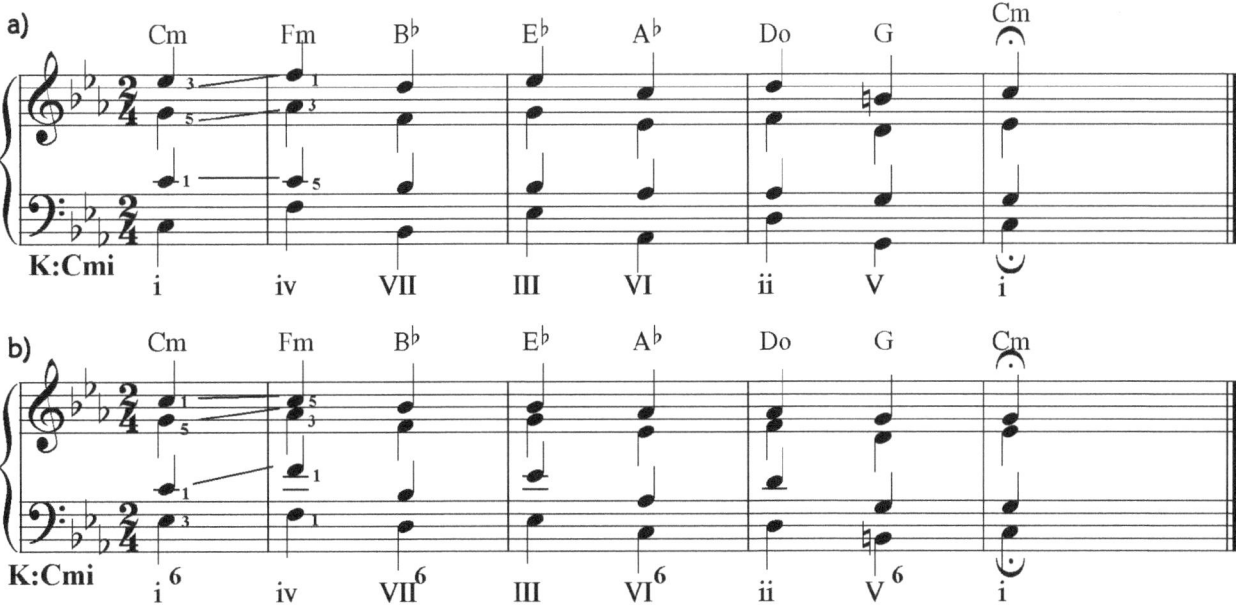

a) Cm   Fm   B♭   E♭   A♭   Do   G   Cm

K:Cmi   i   iv   VII   III   VI   ii   V   i

b) Cm   Fm   B♭   E♭   A♭   Do   G   Cm

K:Cmi   i$^6$   iv   VII$^6$   III   VI$^6$   ii   V$^6$   i

# Root Progressions – Part Three
## Root Movement by Fourths and Fifths

# Part Three B:  Fourth Down (↓4) – Fifth Up (↑5)

Study the following progressions and relate them to the line diagram.

### THE USUAL LOOK

1) How many common notes occur when the two chords appear in root position? ..............

2) Which way do the other upper parts move? ...................................

3) Did you notice that the bass can move either up or down? ......................................

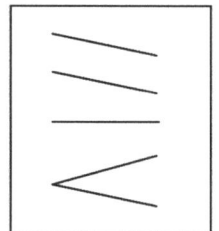

*The upper three part movements can be placed in any voice.*

This is the standard look of the progression
when both chords are in root position.
Other variations may occur when inversions are used.

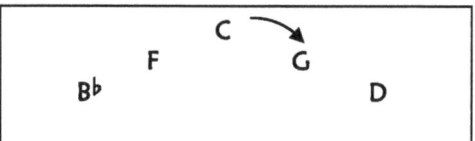

The **root movement** is clockwise around the Cycle of Fifths.

---

**A progression constructed of a series of chords built on roots moving
*down* by a fourth or *up* by a fifth creates *tension*.**

A modern example is *'Lets Do The Time Warp Again'* from the Rocky Horror Show, where only
major chords are placed on a series of root notes, each a fifth higher than the next.

---

### 'Writing Recipe' for the Second Chord When Both Chords are in Root Position

| 4 | ↘ |
| 3 | ↘ |
| 2 | CN |
| 1 | BN |

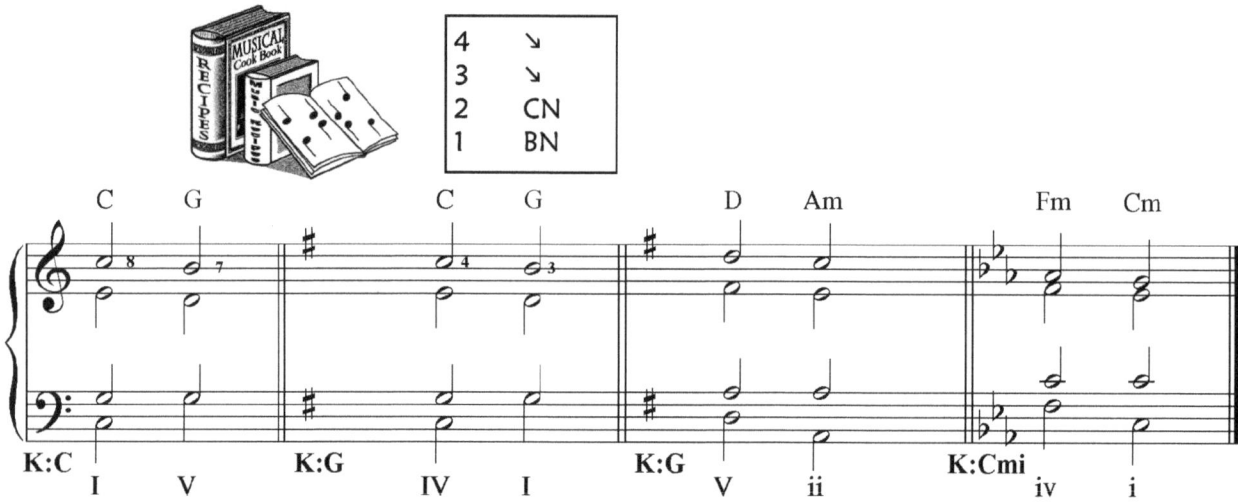

The I – V (i – V) progression can be used
as an intermediary cadence known as an
**Imperfect Cadence** (British)
or **Semicadence.** (American)

The IV-I (iv-i) progression can be used as the
weaker form of a final cadence —
the **Plagal Cadence.**

# Questions: Part Three B (↓4) – (↑5) in Root Position

## Question One

- Write these progressions in a major key using root-position chords.
- Keep the common note in the same part.
- Write the chord symbols over the chords as before.
- Write the bass part going either way, depending on the arrow.
- Track the chord movements on the Chord Table.

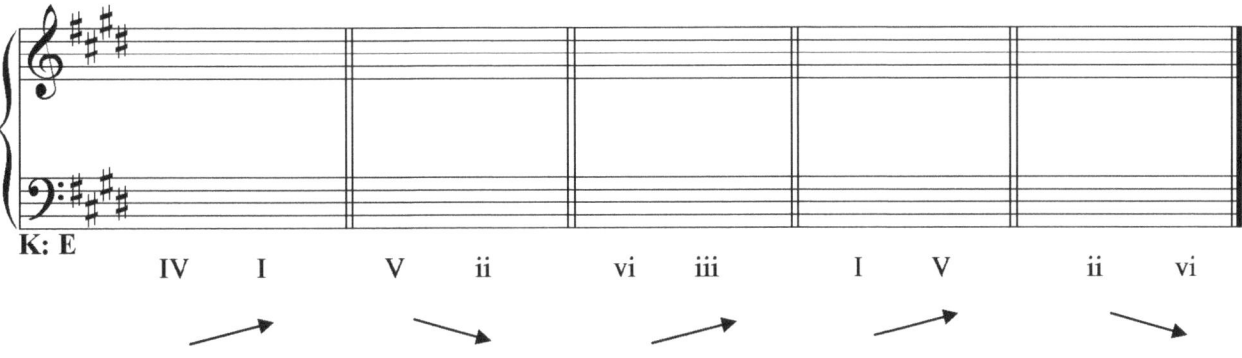

K: E    IV  I    V  ii    vi  iii    I  V    ii  vi

## Question Two

- Write these progressions using root-position chords in a minor key.
- Track the chord movements on the Chord Table.

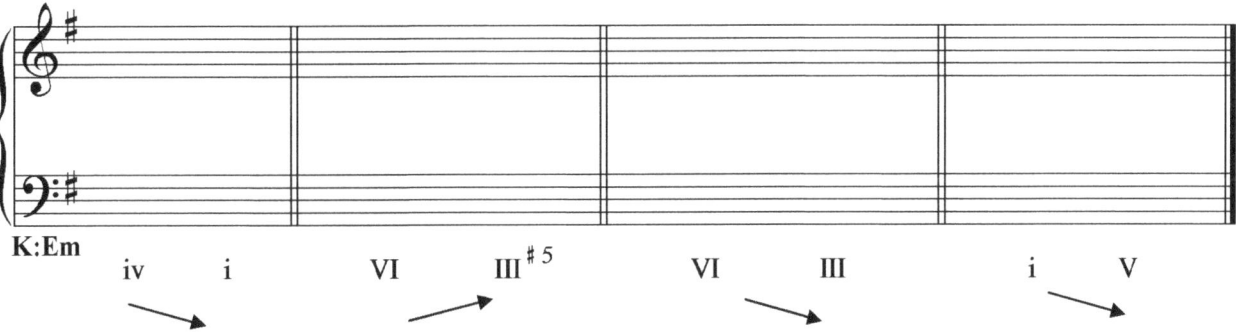

K: Em    iv  i    VI  III#5    VI  III    i  V

## Question Three

The first three bars contain examples of Root Progressions 3B, with unusual movements, that is — with rising melody lines. Colour-code each example to discover the voicings.

- Fill in the inner voices for the remaining bars, 3A and 3B.
- Write more examples of these movements on manuscript.

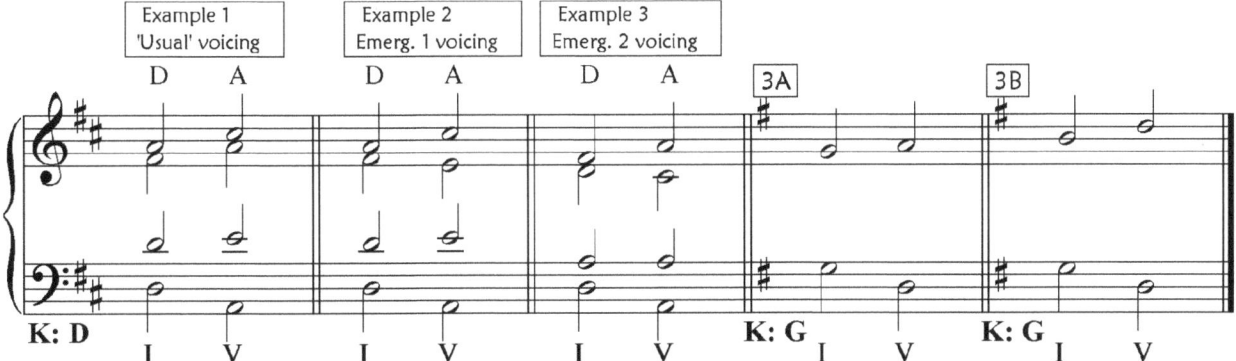

Example 1 'Usual' voicing | Example 2 Emerg. 1 voicing | Example 3 Emerg. 2 voicing | 3A | 3B

K: D   I  V    I  V    I  V    K: G  I  V    K: G  I  V

# Questions: Part Three B (↓4) – (↑5)
## Mixing Root-Position & First-Inversion Chords

Firstly, aim to write the progression using the 'usual' voicing for each chord.
Then, if you have written the two chords correctly and a large leap occurs
in one of the upper three parts, rewrite the progression using **emergency (1)**,
in one of the two chords, to improve the voice-leading and smooth out the gap.

### Question One
- Write these progressions in a major key.
- *Remember to double the third or the fifth in a diminished chord.*

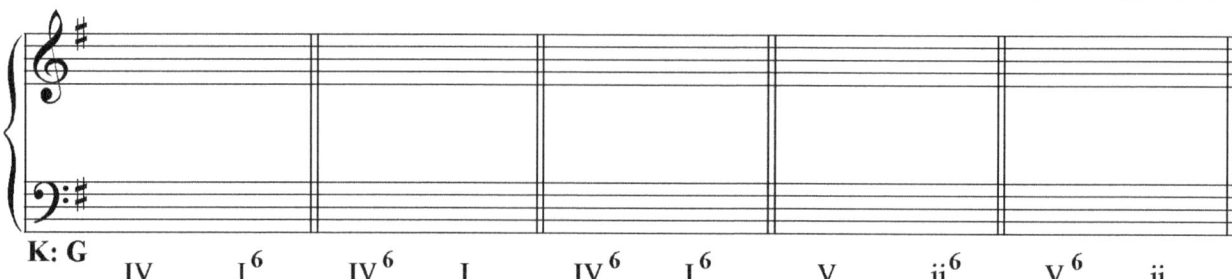

K: G    IV    I$^6$    IV$^6$    I    IV$^6$    I$^6$    V    ii$^6$    V$^6$    ii

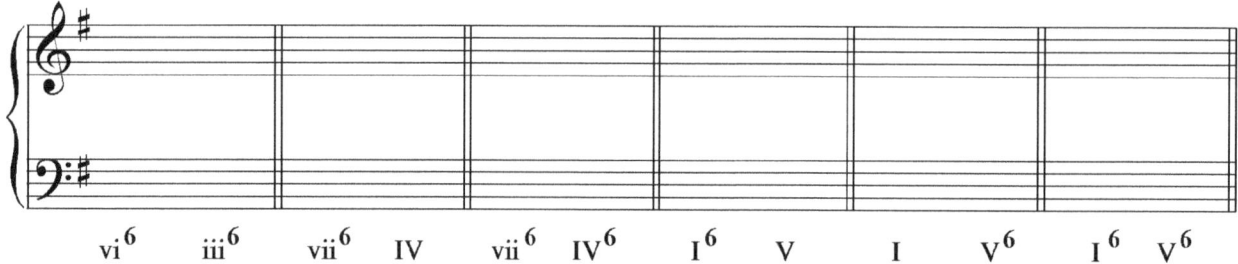

vi$^6$    iii$^6$    vii$^6$    IV    vii$^6$    IV$^6$    I$^6$    V    I    V$^6$    I$^6$    V$^6$

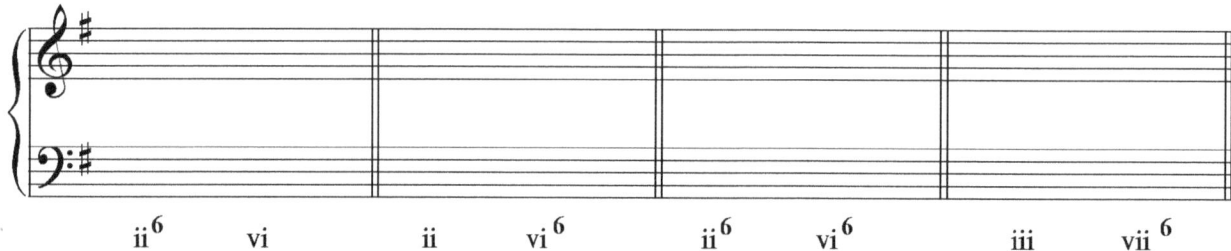

ii$^6$    vi    ii    vi$^6$    ii$^6$    vi$^6$    iii    vii$^6$

### Question Two — An extended progression using Root Progressions: 1, 2B, 3A and 3B
- Write the upper three parts of this progression.
- Indicate the Root Progressions beneath the staff.

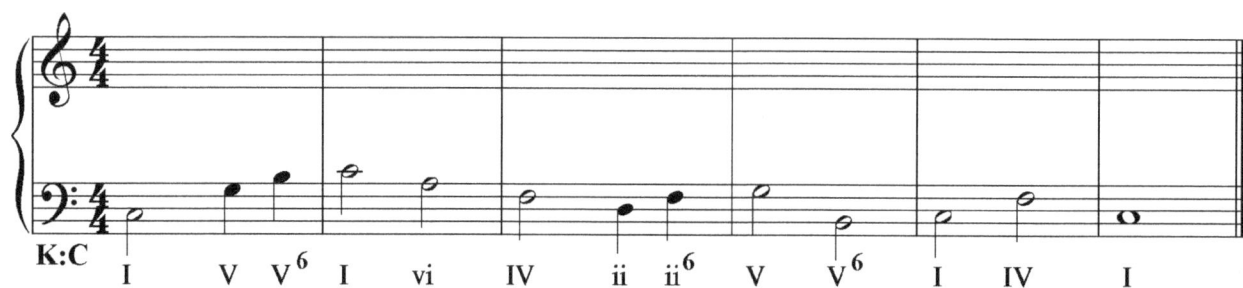

K: C    I    V    V$^6$    I    vi    IV    ii    ii$^6$    V    V$^6$    I    IV    I

# More Questions: Part Three B (↓4) – (↑5)

 **Special Care for the Leading Note in a Minor Key**
1. Take care **not** to double the **leading note** (L.N.)
2. Approach the L.N. from *above*, to avoid creating an Aug 2nd or Aug 4th in a melodic line.

## Question Three

- Write these progressions in a **minor** key working in the same manner as for Q.1

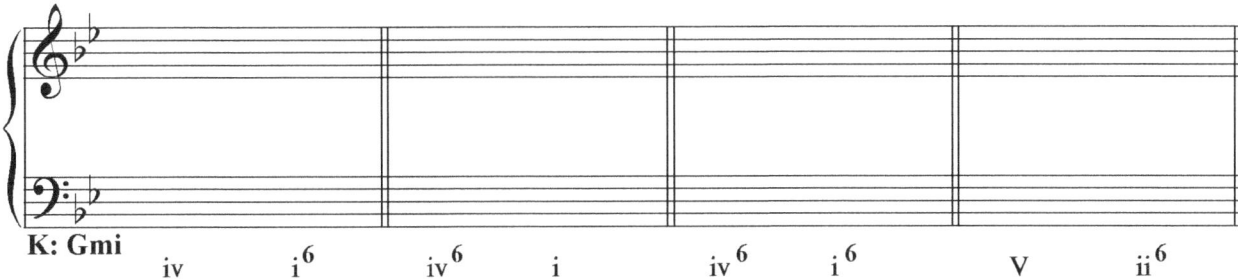

K: Gmi   iv   i⁶   iv⁶   i   iv⁶   i⁶   V   ii⁶

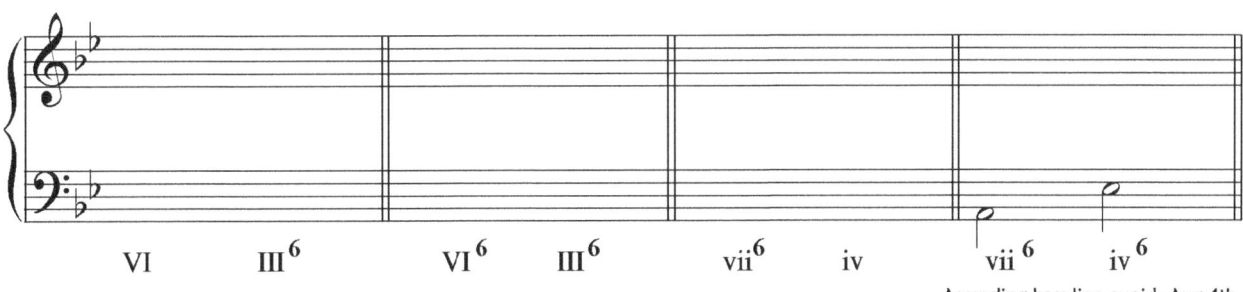

VI   III⁶   VI⁶   III⁶   vii⁶   iv   vii⁶   iv⁶

Ascending bass line avoids Aug 4th

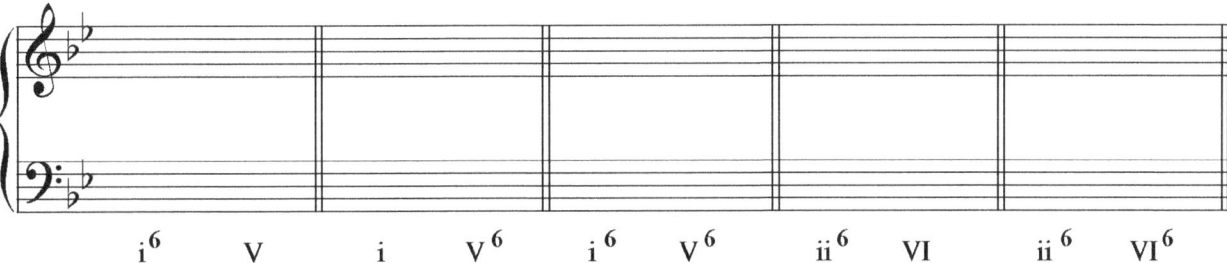

i⁶   V   i   V⁶   i⁶   V⁶   ii⁶   VI   ii⁶   VI⁶

## Question Four

- Write this sequential progression using the rising fifth (falling fourth) root progression in **piano style**.
- Continue the interval pattern established in the first two bars.
- Play the progression and listen to the feeling of tension created by this series of chords.

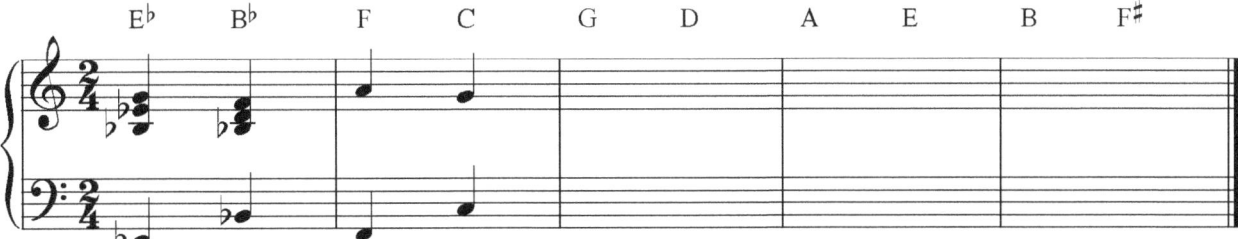

E♭   B♭   F   C   G   D   A   E   B   F♯

Two popular tunes which use this progression are:
1) *Here Comes the Sun* by George Harrison
2) *Let's Do The Time Warp Again* from the Rocky Horror Show

# Root Progressions – Part Four

## Root Movement by Seconds and Sevenths

## Part Four A:   Second Up (↑2) – Seventh Down (↓7)

Any progression in which two root-position chords move by step, must receive
*special attention* so as to avoid consecutive (parallel) P8's and P5's.

> The effect of these stepping progressions is quite strong; it tends to push the harmony forward.
> A satisfying feeling of movement is created owing to the absence of common notes.
> The progression is particularly effective as *contrary motion* between the outside parts is the
> usual movement when the bass is written ↑2.  Movement by ↓7 in the bass is infrequent.

THE USUAL LOOK for progressions:   **I – ii,   iii – IV** (major key only)
**IV – V** or **iv – V** in root position

1) How many common notes occur when the two chords appear in root position? ...............

2) Which way do the upper parts move? ...................................

3) Which way does the bass move ? ........................................

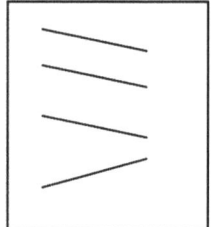

*The upper three part movements can be placed in any voice.*

This is the standard look of the progression
when both chords are in Root Position.
Other variations may occur when inversions are used.

---

'Writing Recipe' for the Second Chord When Both Chords are in Root Position

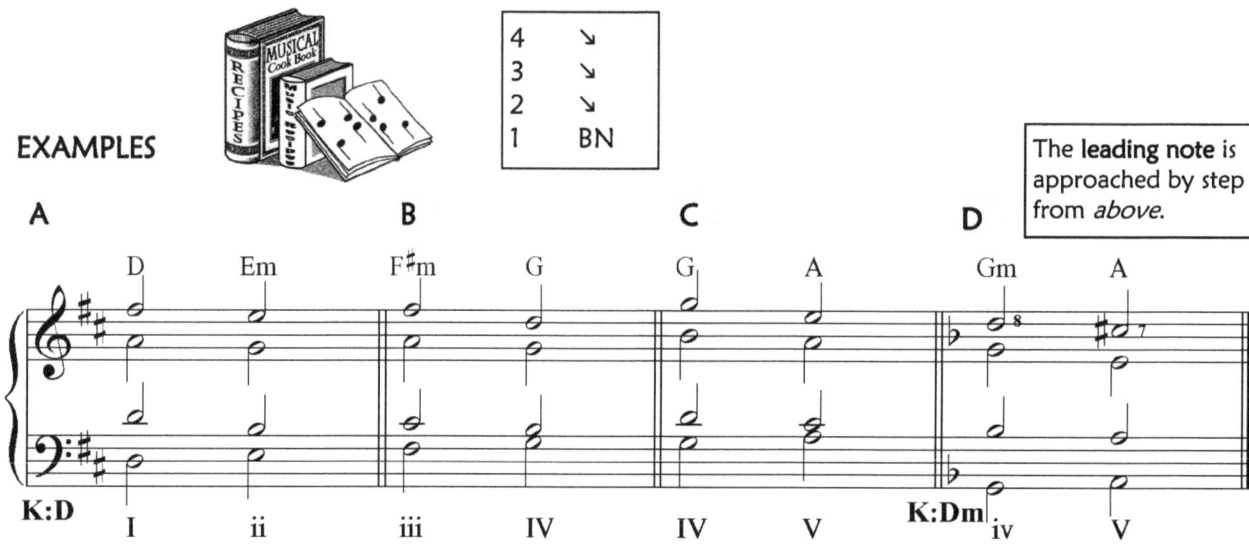

Examples C and D can be used as an
**Imperfect Cadence** (British)
or **Semicadence**. (American)

# Root Movement by Seconds and Sevenths

## The V– vi, V– VI progression

This progression is treated in an exclusive fashion:

- The **third** degree is doubled in chord **VI** to facilitate the movement and aid in the avoidance of consecutive P5's and P8's. (*Emergency 3 voicing*)
- The **leading note (tone)** must *rise* which forces chord **vi (VI)** to have a doubled third.
- Look for the L.N. of the **key** in chord **V** and resolve it to the tonic degree of the key, (which appears as the third degree in chord **vi (VI)**.
- *Colour-code all chords on pages 57 and 58 to discover the doubled notes.*

---

**THE USUAL LOOK** for progressions:

**V– vi** (major key)   **V-VI** (minor key)

1) How many parts move up, including the bass part ? ...............

2) How many parts move down ? ...................................

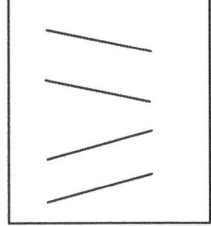

*The upper three part movements can be placed in any voice.*

This is the standard look of the progression
when both chords are in Root Position.
Other variations may occur when inversions are used.

---

### 'Writing Recipe' for the Second Chord When Both Chords are in Root Position

### EXAMPLES

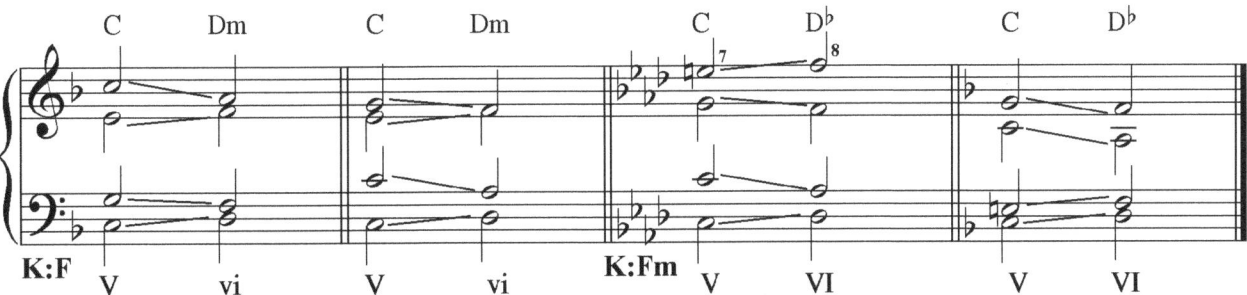

The **V – vi, V—VI** progression can be used as an intermediary cadence    The **leading note** rises.
known as the **Deceptive, Interrupted** or **Surprise Cadence.**

# Questions: Part Four A (↑2) – (↓7)

### Question One
- Write these progressions in a major key using all root-position chords.
- Write the Bass Voice ↑ 2. (Refer to the models on the previous page.)
- \* Remember to double the third degree in chord **vi.**

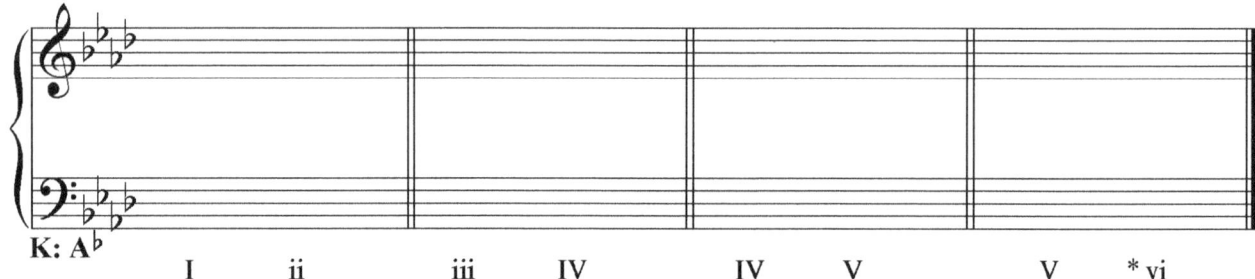

K: A♭   I   ii   iii   IV   IV   V   V   \*vi

### Question Two
- Write these progressions using root-position chords in a **minor** key. (Bass Voice ↑ 2)
- \* Remember to double the third of the chord in chord **VI**

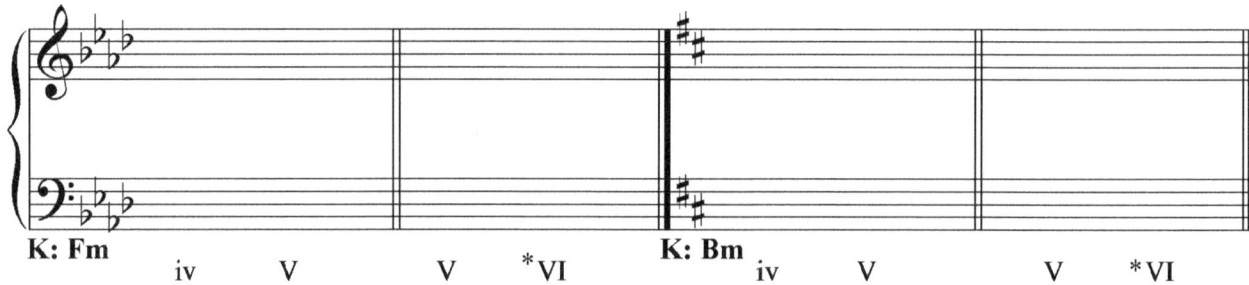

K: Fm   iv   V   V   \*VI    K: Bm   iv   V   V   \*VI

---

**Tips for Writing a Mix of Root-Position & First-Inversion Chords in a Rising Second Root Progression**

- Progressions in which one of the chords is placed in an **inversion** are less likely to have the problem of consecutive octaves and fifths.
- Occasionally chord **vi (VI)** does not require the doubled 3rd.
- Included amongst these are those progressions which use chord **vii⁶** of the key (a diminished chord). For instance **VI** to **vii⁶** or **vii⁶** to **VI**
- **STICKY SITUATION** *Rescue Card tips* (p30), are very useful when writing these progressions.

---

### Question Three – part a
- Write these progressions in a major key. (Write the chord table on page 59.)
- **Take special care when both chords are in first inversion.** You may need to use an emergency voicing in one of the chords in order to avoid consecutive P5's or P8's.

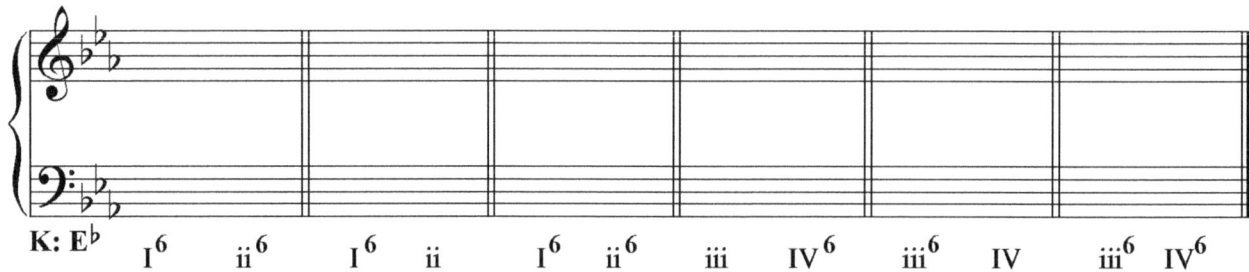

K: E♭   I⁶   ii⁶   I⁶   ii   I⁶   ii⁶   iii   IV⁶   iii⁶   IV   iii⁶   IV⁶

# More Questions: Part Four A (↑2) – (↓7)

**Question Three — part b**

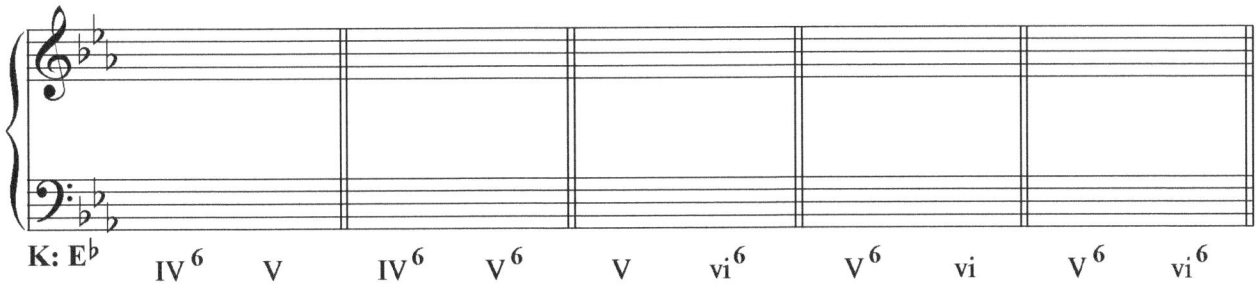

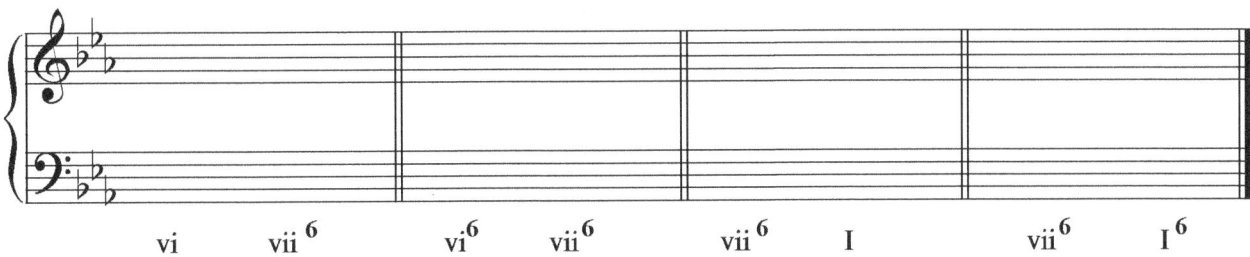

**Question Four**
- Write these progressions in a minor key.
- Take care to avoid **augmented 2nd** and **augmented 4th** intervals in any of the melodic lines.
- These intervals are likely to occur when the **raised 7th** degree appears in one of the chords.

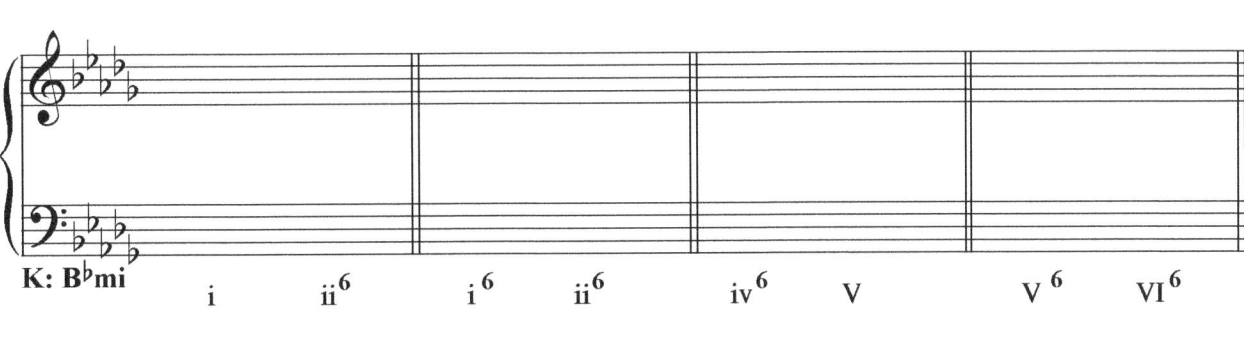

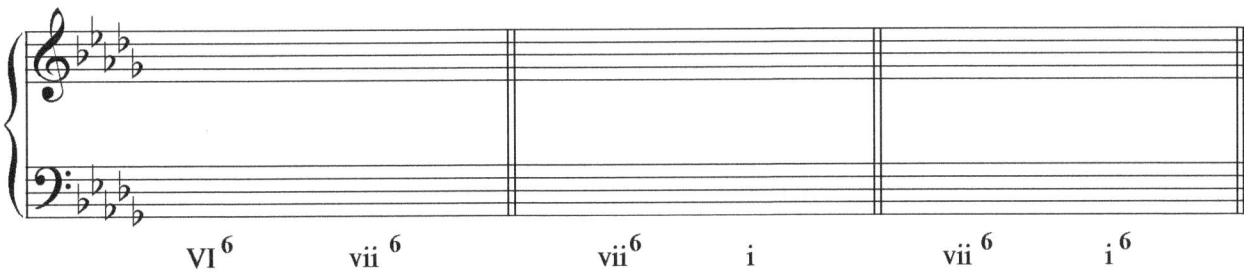

# Root Movement by Seconds and Sevenths

## Part Four B: Second Down (↓2) – Seventh Up (↑7)

- The **downward stepping** root movement has a somewhat weaker effect than the upward moving progression.
- Usually the bass part is best written down a step than up a seventh.
- The **V- IV** progression is considered a weak progression in classical harmony. However, it is effective when used in the more modern **Twelve–Bar Blues** progression.

> **THE USUAL LOOK** for progressions:
> ii—I ,    V– IV  (major key)
> V—iv  (minor key)

1) How many common notes occur when the two chords appear in root position? ..............

2) Which way do the upper parts move? ...................................

3) Which way does the bass move ? .......................................

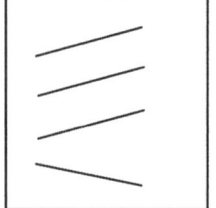

The upper three part movements can be placed in any voice.

This is the standard look of the progression when both chords are in Root Position.
Other variations may occur when inversions are used.

---

### 'Writing Recipe' for the Second Chord When Both Chords are in Root Position

**EXAMPLES**

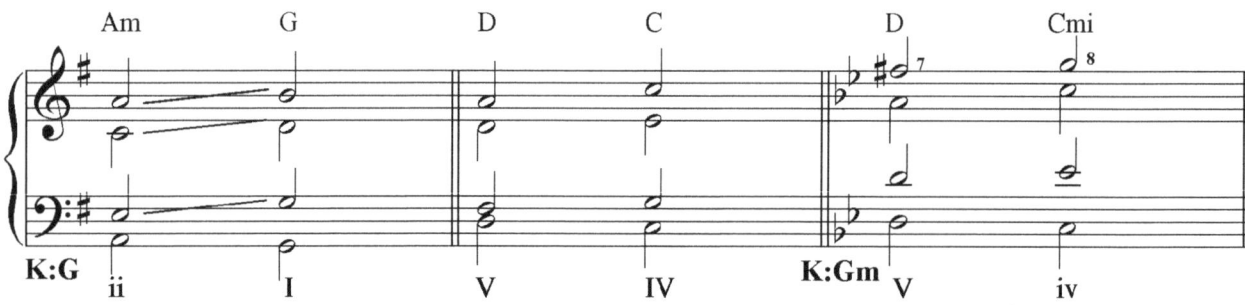

The **leading note** is quitted by (left by) a *half step*.

# Root Movement by Seconds and Sevenths

## The vi–V, VI–V progression

- This progression is treated in a similar fashion to the V–vi (VI) progression.
- In a minor key the third is **always** doubled in chord VI (vi).
- In a major key, the third may be doubled in chord vi, but sometimes it is not.
- *See the excerpt from Bach Chorale 102 for an example of the use of doubled root notes for both chords V and vi in a major key.*
- Colour-code all the chords on this page to discover the settings used.

**THE USUAL LOOK** for progressions:
vi–V (major key), VI-V (minor key)

1) How many parts move down, including the bass part? ...............

2) How many parts move up? ...................................

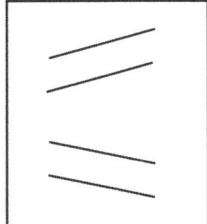

*The upper three part movements can be placed in any voice.*

This is the standard look of the progression
when both chords are in Root Position.
Other variations may occur when inversions are used.

---

### 'Writing Recipe' for the Second Chord When Both Chords are in Root Position

| | |
|---|---|
| 4 | ↗ |
| 3 | ↗ |
| 2 | 8↘7 |
| 1 | BN |

A rather unusual treatment of the vi- V progression.
This excerpt from Bach Chorale 102 is an example of the vi-V progression using doubled root notes for both chords.

**EXAMPLES**

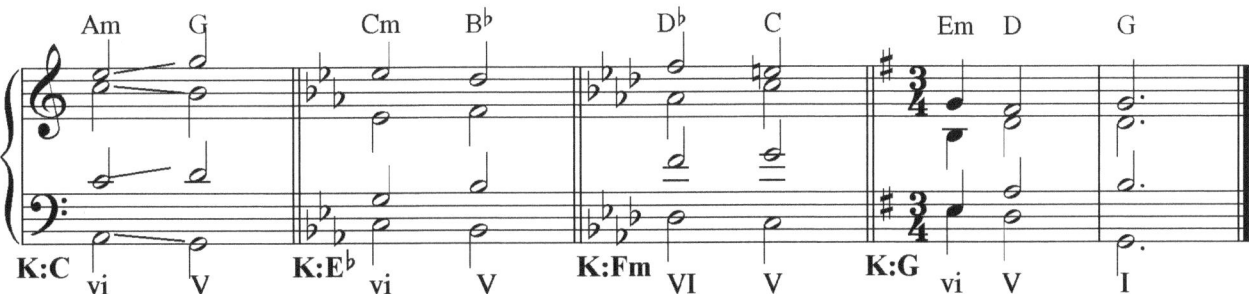

K:C  vi  V    K:E♭ vi  V    K:Fm VI  V    K:G vi  V  I

The vi – V (VI—V) progression can be used as
another version of the intermediary cadence
known as the **Imperfect Cadence or Semi-cadence**.

# Questions: Part Four B (↓2) – (↑7)

 *Write chord tables for each key, either on this page or in a separate workbook.*

### Question One
- Write these progressions in a **major** key using all root-position chords.
- Write the Bass voice down by step. (Refer to the models on the previous page.)

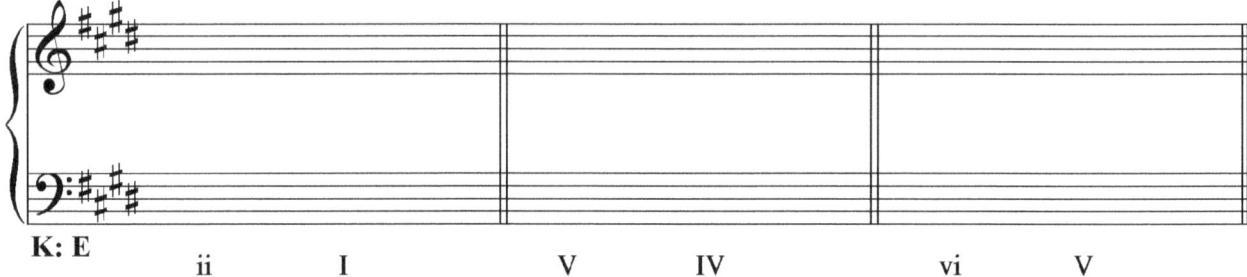

K: E    ii   I    V   IV    vi   V

### Question Two
- Write these progressions using root-position chords in a **minor** key.
- * Remember to double the third of chord **VI**.

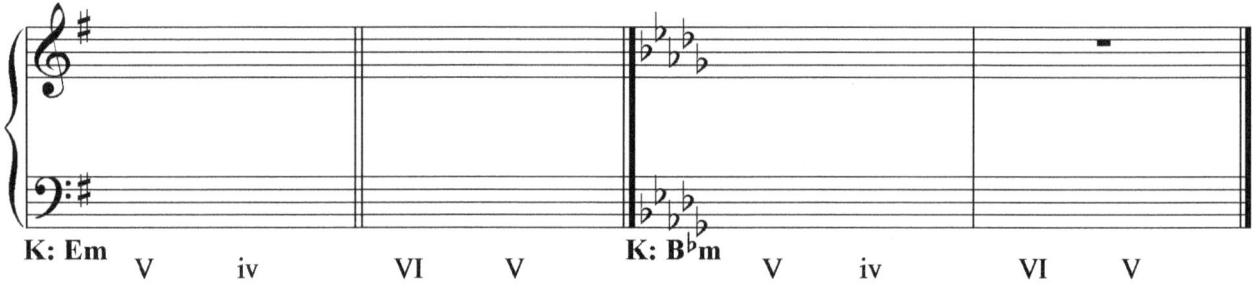

K: Em   V   iv   VI   V    K: B♭m   V   iv   VI   V

---

### Harmony Comes Together —Extended Progression using RP 1, 2A, 2B, 3A, 3B, 4A and 4B
- Write the bass line and the inner parts below the given melody.

K: G    I   ii   I⁶   IV   V   vi   ii   V   V⁶   I   I⁶ vii⁶ I

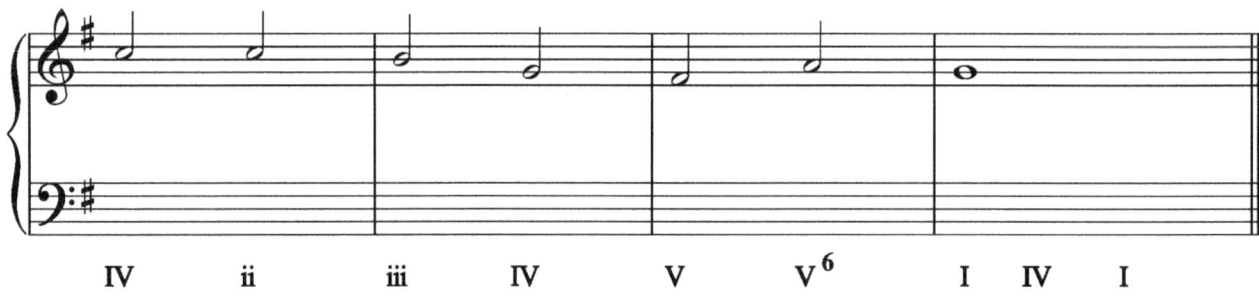

IV   ii   iii   IV   V   V⁶   I   IV   I

# Questions: Part Four B (↓2) – (↑7)
## Mixing Root-Position & First-Inversion Chords

 *Write chord tables for each key, either on this page or in a separate workbook.*

### Question Three
- Write these progressions in a major key.

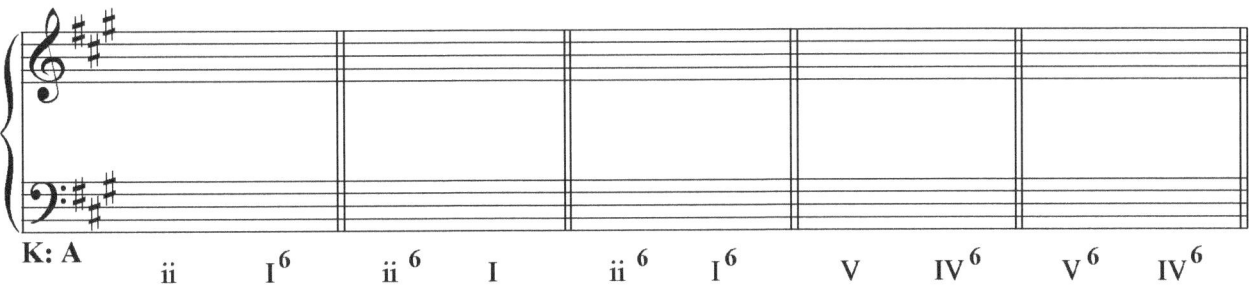

K: A    ii    I⁶    ii⁶    I    ii⁶    I⁶    V    IV⁶    V⁶    IV⁶

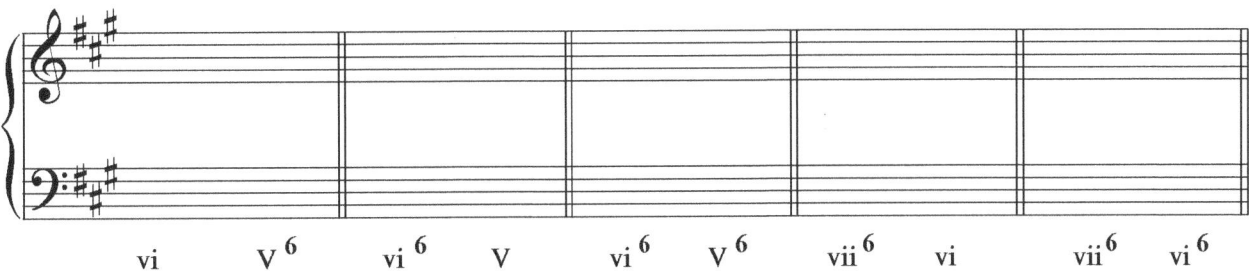

vi    V⁶    vi⁶    V    vi⁶    V⁶    vii⁶    vi    vii⁶    vi⁶

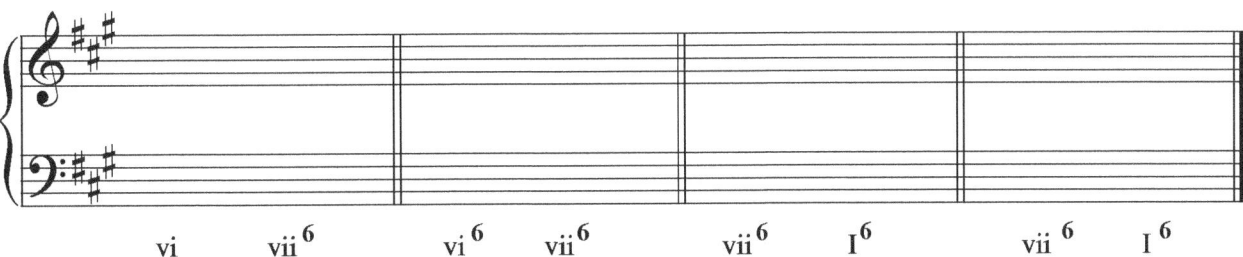

vi    vii⁶    vi⁶    vii⁶    vii⁶    I⁶    vii⁶    I⁶

### Question Four
- Write these progressions in a minor key working in the same manner as before.
- Take care to avoid Aug 2nd and Aug 4th intervals in any of the melodic lines.

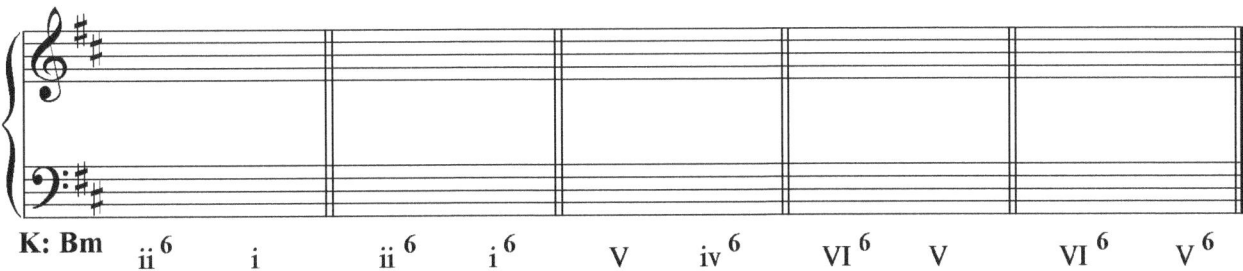

K: Bm    ii⁶    i    ii⁶    i⁶    V    iv⁶    VI⁶    V    VI⁶    V⁶

# How to Write a Series of First-Inversion Chords in a Major Key

- When writing a series of first-inversion chords, care must be taken to avoid consecutive P5's and P8's.
- The solution is to double the **root note** in one chord, and the **fifth degree** in the following chord.
- If the diminished chord (vii°) occurs, try to make sure that the **fifth** is the degree that is doubled in this chord.
- As the series is a sequence, a diminished chord in root position with a doubled root note may be used, although it has a more dissonant sound than when the chord is voiced with a doubled fifth.

---

### 'Writing recipe' for this progression

- Place a series of **roots** in the *soprano* voice.
- Place a series of **fifths** in the *alto* voice.
- Place the **third** of each chord in the *bass* voice.
- Place an **alternating series of roots and fifths** in the *tenor* voice.
- *Question one provides a model.*

## Question One
- Name each chord.
- Colour-code every chord to discover the voicings.

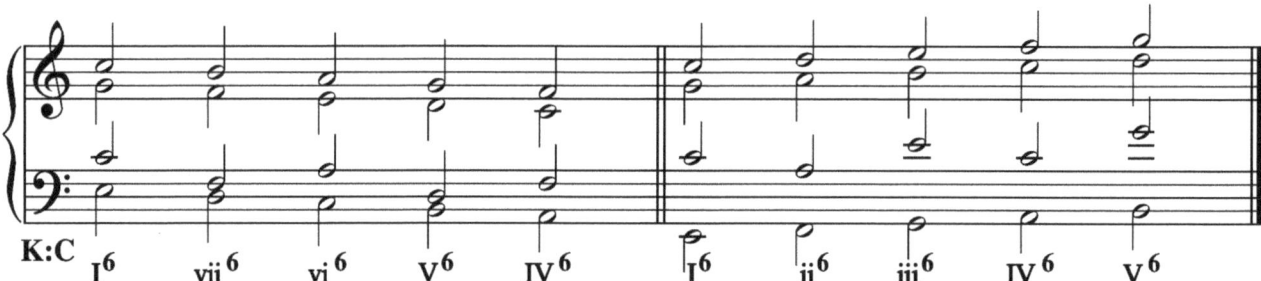

K:C  I⁶  vii⁶  vi⁶  V⁶  IV⁶   I⁶  ii⁶  iii⁶  IV⁶  V⁶

## Question Two
- Complete the upper three voices for this series of first-inversion chords resolving onto a final root-position chord.

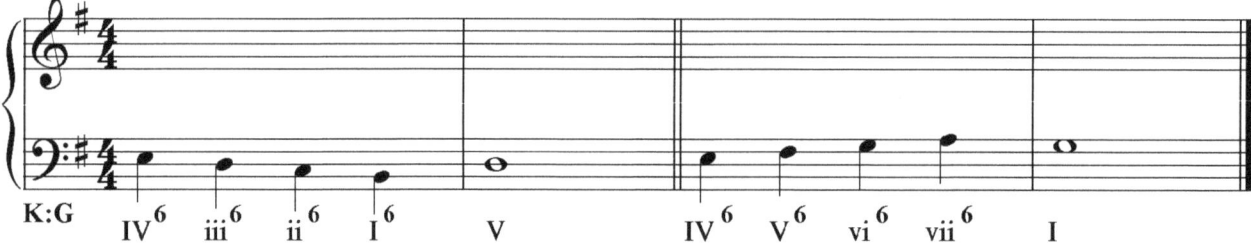

K:G  IV⁶  iii⁶  ii⁶  I⁶  V   IV⁶  V⁶  vi⁶  vii⁶  I

# Common Progressions using Three Chords

**Question One**
- Complete the inner voices (tenor & alto) for these progressions.

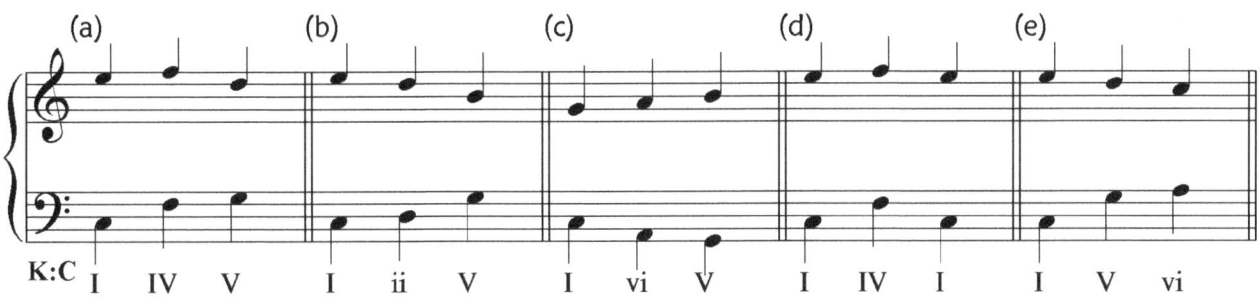

K:C
(a) I  IV  V
(b) I  ii  V
(c) I  vi  V
(d) I  IV  I
(e) I  V  vi

(f) I  iii  IV
(g) I  iii  vi
(h) vi  IV  V
(i) vi  ii  V

**Question Two**
- Complete the inner voices for these progressions which use a mixture of root-position and first-inversion chords.

K:C
(a) I⁶  I  V
(b) I  I⁶  I
(c) I  V⁶  I
(d) I⁶  IV  I⁶

(e) I  I⁶  V
(f) I  I⁶  V
(g) V  I⁶  I
(h) I⁶  vii⁶  I

(i) I  vii⁶  I⁶
(j) I  ii⁶  V
(k) I  IV⁶  V
(l) I  vi⁶  V⁶

**Use of the Diminished Chord:** Progressions (h) and (i) occur frequently in the opening phrase of a piece. If written correctly, alternating Perfect 5ths and Diminished 5ths will occur in the tenor and alto voices.

# Root Progressions – Part Five

## Root Progressions in *Action*...

**Play, listen to and analyse the excerpts from the Bach Chorales in major keys, to experience the effect of the various Root Progressions.**

For all the chorale analyses on the next few pages follow this procedure:
1. Write a chord table for each key
2. Indicate the modern chord names for each chord
3. Write the degree number and figuring for the inversions below the bass part, omitting any passing notes
4. Indicate the Root Progressions above the chord symbols with red arrows
   You can indicate the progression either way;  eg ↑5 or ↓4, ↑3 or ↓6
5. Complete the exercise by colour-coding the chords to discover the settings

| Example of how to indicate the Root Progressions | | | | | | | |
|---|---|---|---|---|---|---|---|
| **Root Prog:** | ↑5 | ↑2 | ↑5 | ↑2 | ↓3 | ↓5 | ↓5 |
| **Chord Name:** C | G | Am | Em | F | Dm | G | C |

- *Once each exercise is completed, assess how many strong movements (4ths, 5ths & 2nds) and how many weaker movements (3rds, 6ths) were used . Also look at the beat of the bar (measure) in which they occur.*
- *Relate each one to the previous sections on Root Progressions and track the journey of the progressions on the chord table.*
- *Discuss the movements with your teacher.*

| Primary Root Movement Progressions Summary | Secondary Root Movement Progressions Summary |
|---|---|
| 1)   ↑4 -↓5 | |
| 2)   ↑2 -↓7 | 1)   ↓4 -↑5 |
| 3)   ↓3 -↑6 | 2)   ↓2 -↑7 |

## Question One

**Wach'auf, mein Herz** (first four bars)

No. 93 from 371 Harmonised Chorales by J.S.Bach

- The figuring for four-note chords (7ths) and the suspension has been done for you.
  (Refer to *Contemporary Theory Workbook, Bk2* or the *Contemporary Chord Workbook—Bk 1*, for information on the figuring for 7th chords)
- Progressions using these chords will be explored later in this series.

Reminder:  the Root Progression is assessed from the name of the chord which is not necessarily in the bass voice.

4 - 3 Suspension
See Book 2

# Root Progressions in *Action*...

### Question Two
**Jesu nun sie gepreiset** – simplified version (last four bars)

No. 11 from 371 Harmonised Chorales by J.S.Bach

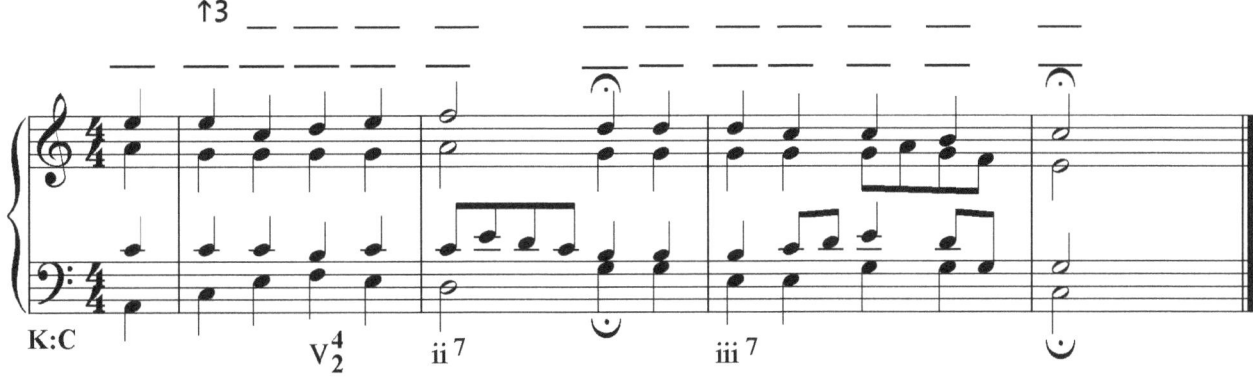

### Question Three
**O Herre Gott, dein gottlich Wort** (first five bars)

No. 14 from 371 Harmonised Chorales by J.S.Bach

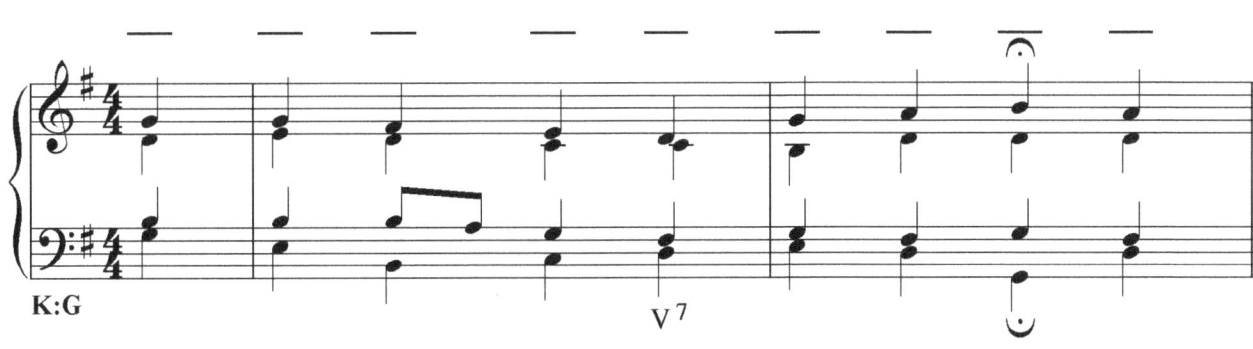

## Summary of the Root Position and First-Inversion Chords Readily Available in Major and Minor Keys

|  | MAJOR | MINOR |
|---|---|---|
| Root Position | IV  I  V<br>ii  vi  iii | iv  i  V<br>VI  III |
| First Inversion | $IV^6$  $I^6$  $V^6$<br>$ii^6$  $vi^6$  $iii^6$<br>$vii^6$ | $iv^6$  $i^6$  $V^6$<br>$VI^6$  $(III+^6)$  $ii^6$<br>$vii^6$ |

**Remember** — diminished chords are rarely used in root position, owing to the harsh sound. They are only used in special circumstances, for instance - in a sequence. (cf Bach Chorale 26, bar 7) The augmented chord in first inversion requires special treatment, which is why it is bracketed.

### Question Four
- Complete the inner voices of this progression.
- Revise the previous pages to help you remember the 'writing recipes' for the various types of Root Progressions.

K:C  I  $vii^6$  $I^6$  IV  V  vi  iii  vi  ii  V  I

### Question Five
- Complete the inner voices of this progression.
- Refer to page 44 for ways to treat the **V-I** progression in the final bar.

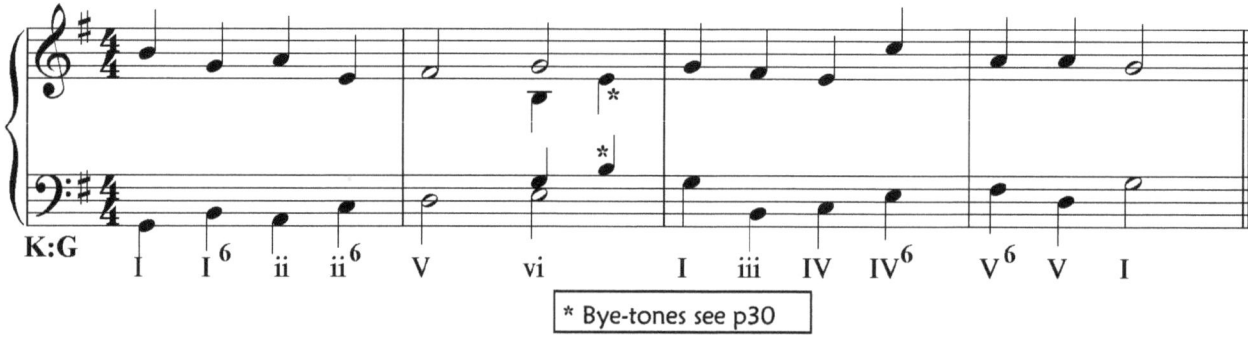

K:G  I  $I^6$  ii  $ii^6$  V  vi  I  iii  IV  $IV^6$  $V^6$  V  I

* Bye-tones see p30

# Play, Listen to & Analyse the Excerpts from Chorales in Minor Keys

## Question Six

**Herzliebster Jesu, was hast du (first three bars)**

No. 78 from 371 Harmonised Chorales by J.S.Bach

- *Note the use of the raised 6th and 7th from the melodic minor scale*
  *- the ascending form used in a descending line!*

## Question Seven

**Da der Herr Christ zu Tische saß.**

No. 196 from 371 Harmonised Chorales by J.S.Bach

## Question Eight

- This example in the style of a Bach Chorale, makes use of the augmented triad.

# Chord Progressions in Minor Keys

- Complete the inner voices of these progressions.
- Indicate the Root Progressions.
- Track the journey of each progression on the Chord Table for the key.

**Question Nine**

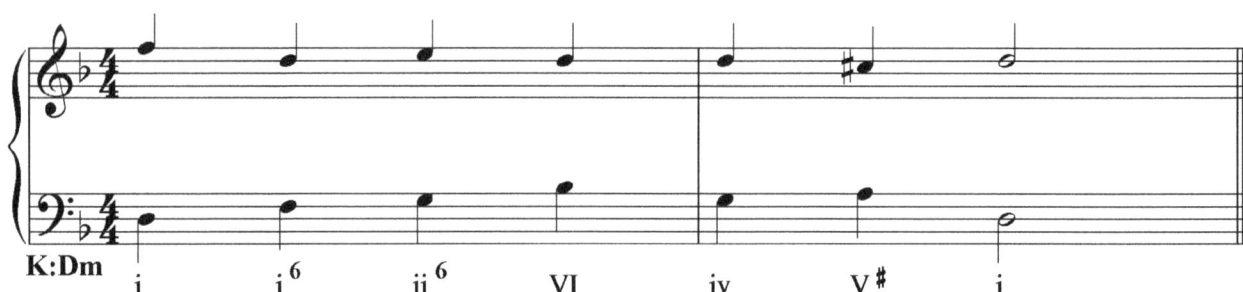

K:Dm   i   i$^6$   ii$^6$   VI   iv   V$^\sharp$   i

**Question Ten**

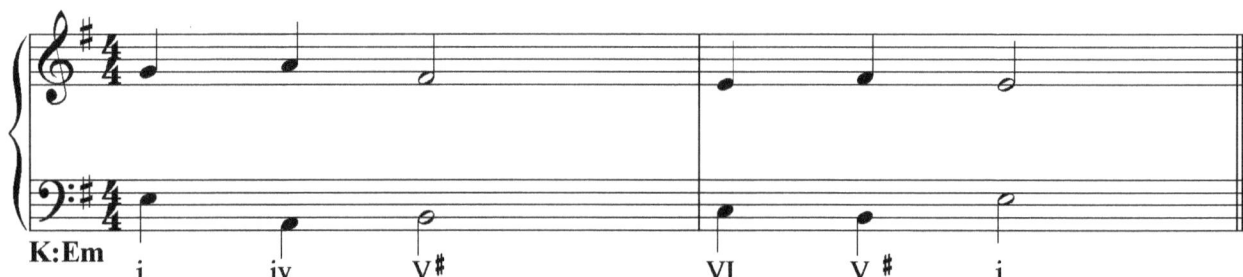

K:Em   i   iv   V$^\sharp$   VI   V$^\sharp$   i

**Question Eleven**

Chord **III** is taken from the descending melodic minor scale.

K:Gm   i   III   iv   V$^\sharp$   ii$^6$   V$^\sharp$   i

# Harmony Comes Together!

Applied Analysis using Root-Position and First-Inversion Chords

## Aura Lee — version one

Here is our first setting of the folk tune 'Aura Lee' using only root-position and first-inversion chords. Other versions using more chord choices will appear in the next book in this series.

1. Write a chord table for the key
2. Indicate the modern chord names for each chord
3. Write the degree number and figuring for the inversions below the bass part, omitting any passing notes
4. Colour-code the chords to discover the settings
5. Play the example, listening closely to the effect of the chord progressions

> *Later in this series, we will see and hear other settings of Aura Lee.*
> *You can then compare the sounds on this page to those created*
> *when the tune is harmonised with second-inversion chords*
> *and later again when it is harmonised with various types of seventh chords.*

Question Twelve

### Aura Lee

# Root Progressions – Review Exercises

> Complete these review exercises in a separate manuscript book over a period of time, as you continue to progress to the following lessons on cadences.

## Section One — Root - Position Chords

### Question One
- On a separate page, create a summary of the line diagrams for each of the root movements.
- Refer to your summary as you complete questions 2—5.

### Question Two
- Pay *special attention* to these progressions which move by step.

| | | |
|---|---|---|
| ↑ 2 | a) Key D | I — ii,    iii—IV,    IV—V,    V—vi |
| ↑ 2 | b) Key Dm | iv — V,    V—VI |
| ↓ 2 | c) Key G | vi—V |
| ↓ 2 | d) Key Gm | VI— V |

### Question Three

| | | |
|---|---|---|
| ↑3 or ↓6 | a) Key F | ii — IV,    IV—vi,    vi—I |
| ↑3 or ↓6 | b) Key Fm | iv — VI,    VI— i |
| ↓3 or ↑6 | c) Key A | I — vi,    IV—ii,    vi—IV |
| ↓3 or ↑6 | d) Key Am | i — VI,    VI— iv |

### Question Four

| | | |
|---|---|---|
| ↑4 or ↓5 | a) Key B♭ | I — IV,    ii—V,    iii—vi,    V—I,    vi—ii |
| ↑4 or ↓5 | b) Key B♭m | i — iv,    V— i |
| ↓4 or ↑5 | c) Key G | I — V,    ii—vi,    IV— I,    V—ii |
| ↓4 or ↑5 | d) Key Gm | i — V,    iv— i |

### Question Five — longer mixed root progressions

| | | | | | |
|---|---|---|---|---|---|
| a) Key E | I—ii —V | ii —V—I, | ii—I—V, | ii—V—vi | ii—IV—I, |
| b) Key B | I— IV —V | IV—V—I, | IV—V—vi, | | |
| c) Key Em | i — iv —V | iv—V— i, | iv—V—VI, | | |
| d) Key E♭ | vi—V—I | | | | |
| e) Key Cm | VI—V—i | | | | |

# Root Progressions – Review Exercises

## Section Two — Root-Position and First-Inversion Chords

*Remember that progressions which include first inversion chords do not follow the standard models that apply to progressions using only root position chords.*

### Question One

| | | | |
|---|---|---|---|
| ↑ 2 | a) Key G | $I^6$ — ii,   I— $ii^6$,   $IV^6$—V,   $V^6$—$vi^6$,   $vi^6$—$vii^6$,   $vii^6$—I,   $vii^6$—$I^6$ |
| ↑ 2 | b) Key Fm | i— $ii^6$,   $iv^6$—V,   $vii^6$—i,   $vii^6$—$i^6$ |
| ↓ 2 | c) Key D | $ii^6$—I,   $ii^6$—$I^6$,   $vi^6$—V,   $vi^6$—$V^6$,   $vii^6$—vi |
| ↓ 2 | d) Key B♭m | $ii^6$—i,   $ii^6$—$i^6$,   $VI^6$—V,   $VI^6$—$V^6$,   $vii^6$—VI |

### Question Two

- Write three versions of each progression: $\frac{5}{3}$ to $\frac{6}{3}$ | $\frac{6}{3}$ to $\frac{5}{3}$ | $\frac{6}{3}$ to $\frac{6}{3}$
- Omit any progressions which include a diminished chord in root position.

| | | |
|---|---|---|
| ↑3 or ↓6 | a) Key F♯ | ii — IV,   IV—vi,   vi—I |
| ↑3 or ↓6 | b) Key Fm | ii — iv,   iv — VI,   VI— i |
| ↓3 or ↑6 | c) Key A♭ | I — vi,   IV—ii,   vi—IV |
| ↓3 or ↑6 | d) Key Cm | i — VI,   iv— ii,   VI— iv |

### Question Three

- Write three versions of each progression: $\frac{5}{3}$ to $\frac{6}{3}$ | $\frac{6}{3}$ to $\frac{5}{3}$ | $\frac{6}{3}$ to $\frac{6}{3}$
- Omit those progressions which include a diminished chord in root position.

| | | |
|---|---|---|
| ↑4 or ↓5 | a) Key E | I — IV,   ii—V,   iii—vi,   V—I,   vi—ii |
| ↑4 or ↓5 | b) Key Em | i — iv,   V— i |
| ↓4 or ↑5 | c) Key G♭ | I — V,   ii—vi,   IV— I,   V—ii |
| ↓4 or ↑5 | d) Key Fm | i — V,   iv— i |

### Question Four — longer mixed root progressions

| | |
|---|---|
| a) Key A♭ | $ii^6$—V—I,   $ii^6$—IV—I,   $ii^6$—I—V,   $ii^6$—IV—V,   $ii^6$—V—VI |
| b) Key G | $IV^6$—V—I,   $IV^6$—V—vi,   I—$IV^6$—V |
| c) Key Dm | $iv^6$—V—i,   $iv^6$—V—VI, |
| d) Key B | $vi^6$—V—I |
| e) Key Gm | $VI^6$—V—i,   i—$VII^6$—III (from descending melodic minor)   (Use descending melody: - insert PN between last two chords )   ♩ ♪♪ ♩   8– 7-6 -5 |

# Cadences

- The word *cadence* comes from the Latin 'cadere' meaning *to fall*.

- The term is used to describe the progression created by the final two chords at the end of a section of music, where the music comes to either a temporary or a complete rest.

- Places to look for cadences are:
  (i) at the end of a phrase mark
  (ii) or when the second chord is of longer time value, which could often be marked with a *fermata* (pause sign).

- As in language, musical compositions have phrases which divide music into sections.

- In some harmony texts you may see the first phrase of a tune labelled as the '*antecedent phrase*' and the balancing phrase which follows labelled as the '*consequent phrase*'.

- The larger unit made up of both phrases is labelled a '*period*'.

- Certain chord progressions create a feeling of finality, either for a mid-phrase or at a final phrase. They are known as **half close** and **full close** respectively.

- Cadences therefore help define the harmonic structure of music as commas and full stops (periods) do in language and as columns divide and define the spaces of a building.

## A MUSICAL JOURNEY

**A musical composition can be thought of as a journey.**

*A typical journey is as follows...*

The chord progression begins at **home** utilising the **tonic chord** at the beginning of the first full bar. The progression then travels to the *most important destination*, which ends on the dominant chord. From there the progression often travels to a **third section** ending on the **relative major chord** or the **relative minor chord**. Lastly the progression returns to its home finishing on the **tonic** chord of the key.

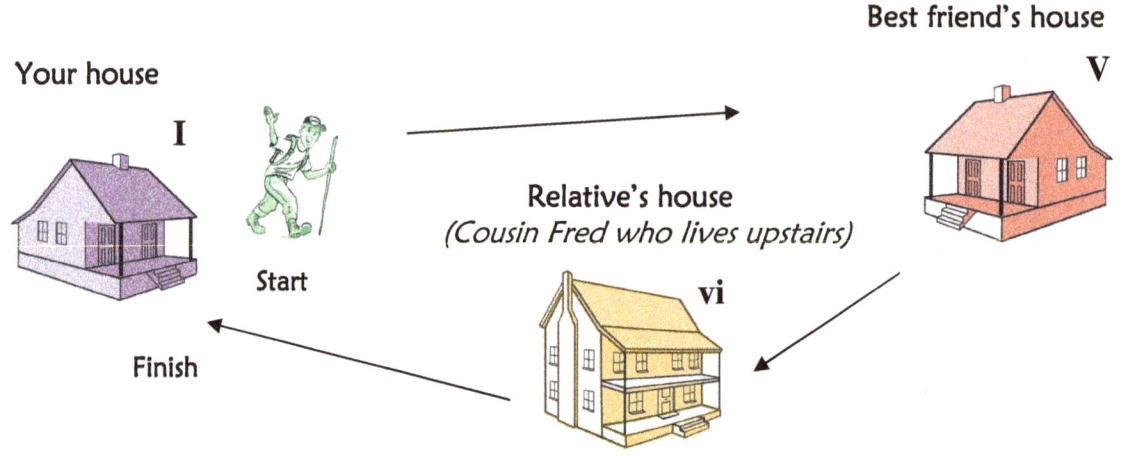

# More Facts about Cadences

## SUMMARY

- Final cadences end on the **tonic chord** of the key. (**I or i**)

- **Intermediary cadences** end on either the **dominant chord (V)** or the **submediant chord (vi or VI)**.

- The most solid cadences place both chords in **root position**.  $\frac{5}{3} - \frac{5}{3}$

- Those cadences with one chord in an inversion are possible but less solid.  $\frac{6}{3} - \frac{5}{3}$
  
  These cadences are sometimes labelled 'medial' or 'inverted'.   OR   $\frac{5}{3} - \frac{6}{3}$

- When both chords are in first inversion, *no* cadence is created.

## Labelling of Cadences in Various Texts

There are four main types of cadences -

1) A **final cadence** labelled **perfect**, **authentic** or **full close**

    In some American texts the *authentic cadence* is further subdivided into sub-categories::
    (a) *perfect* authentic cadences - those ending on the tonic degree in the soprano part (PAC)
    (b) *imperfect* authentic cadences— those ending on either the 3rd or 5th degree in the soprano part. (IAC)

2) A **final cadence** labelled **plagal** or **amen**

3) The **intermediary** cadences are labelled differently in various texts —

    a) In the British system there are four variations of the cadence ending on **V**.
       These are all known as **imperfect cadences**.
    b) In some American texts, cadences ending on V are known as **semi-cadence, demi-cadence, half cadence** or **half close**.

4) The **interrupted cadence** which uses chords **V– vi (V –VI)** is labelled in various ways including — **interrupted, deceptive, surprise, abrupt, avoided, broken** and **evaded**.
   In this book, they will be labelled *interrupted* or *deceptive*..

# Four Types of Cadences

## Final Cadences          Intermediary Cadences

| A Strong final ending | | | C Four types | | |
|---|---|---|---|---|---|
| **Perfect cadence** | V | I | **Imperfect cadence** | I | V |
| (Authentic cadence) | vii⁶ | I | (Semicadence or half cadence) | ii | V |
| (Full close) | | | (Half close) | IV | V |
| | | | | vi | V |
| B Weaker final ending | | | D | | |
| **Plagal cadence** | IV | I | **Interrupted cadence** | V | vi |
| (Amen cadence) | | | (Surprise cadence) | vii⁶ | vi |
| | | | (Deceptive cadence) | | |

*The chord types in the above table are for major keys. Keep in mind that the first chord in each progression is frequently written in first inversion. For instance* **V⁶—I**

**Question One**

- Complete the following chart of cadences in a minor key.
- Adjust the chord types and inversions to suit the minor key.
- Remember that chord ii is a diminished chord, so it is used *only* in first inversion.

| A Strong final ending | | | C Four types | | |
|---|---|---|---|---|---|
| **Perfect cadence** | V | ___ | **Imperfect cadence** | ___ | V |
| (Authentic cadence) | vii⁶ | ___ | (Semicadence or half cadence) | ___ | V |
| (Full close) | | | (Half close) | ___ | V |
| | | | | ___ | V |
| B Weaker final ending | | | D | | |
| **Plagal cadence** | ___ | ___ | **Interrupted cadence** | V | ___ |
| (Amen cadence) | | | (Surprise cadence) | vii⁶ | ___ |
| | | | (Deceptive cadence) | | |

# Where to use Cadences in the Phrase of a Piece

| | Phrase one<br>-in the body of the piece | Phrase two<br>- at the end of a piece | Things to observe |
|---|---|---|---|
| 1 | | ♩ \| 𝅗𝅥<br>Perfect (Authentic) | **PAC**<br>Leading note rises 7 ↗ 8<br>or melody falls 3↘2↘1.<br>(see p78 -80) |
| 2 | | ♩ \| 𝅗𝅥<br>Plagal<br><br>or *Perfect* with a *Plagal* extension<br>♩ \| 𝅗𝅥 𝅗𝅥 \| 𝅝<br>V  I  IV  I<br>Plagal extension | Subdominant degree falls 4 ↘ 3. |
| 3 | ♩ \| 𝅗𝅥<br>Imperfect<br>(Semicadence) | | **IV ( iv )—V** Root prog. ↑2<br><br>**vi (VI) — V** Root prog. ↓2 |
| 4 | ♩ \| 𝅗𝅥<br>Interrupted<br>(Deceptive) | | **V — vi (VI)** Root prog. ↑2 |

**Practical exercises**
- Find examples of cadences in pieces you are playing so that you can *play*, *listen to* and *compare* the effects of the different types of cadences.
- Continue to play the written examples on the following pages, as well as the cadences and chord progressions you write for yourself.

# Perfect Cadence (Authentic Cadence)

*Before commencing these exercises refer to Root Progressions—Part 3A pp42-44*

The root movement in a **perfect cadence (authentic cadence)** is by a rising fourth or falling fifth. As previously stated, root movement by **rising fourths** or **falling fifths** produces a very solid sound of pleasing resolution and is therefore a suitable progression on which to end a piece of music.

The root movement for a **perfect cadence** is *anticlockwise* around the Cycle of Fifths.

The movement can be tracked on the table in this manner: | IV | I ← V |

## Part One—Resolution of a Perfect Cadence where the Melody Rises

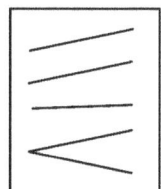

*The upper three part movements can be placed in any voice.*

This is the standard look of the progression
when both chords are in root position.
Other variations may occur when inversions are used.

### Writing Recipe' for the Second Chord When Both Chords are in Root Position

| 4 | Left over note (L/O) ↗ |
| 3 | 7 ↗ 8 |
| 2 | Common Note |
| 1 | Bass Note (BN) |

**Example One :** In the American system this first example is known as a **perfect authentic cadence** as the soprano melody moves from the leading note (7) to the upper tonic (8).

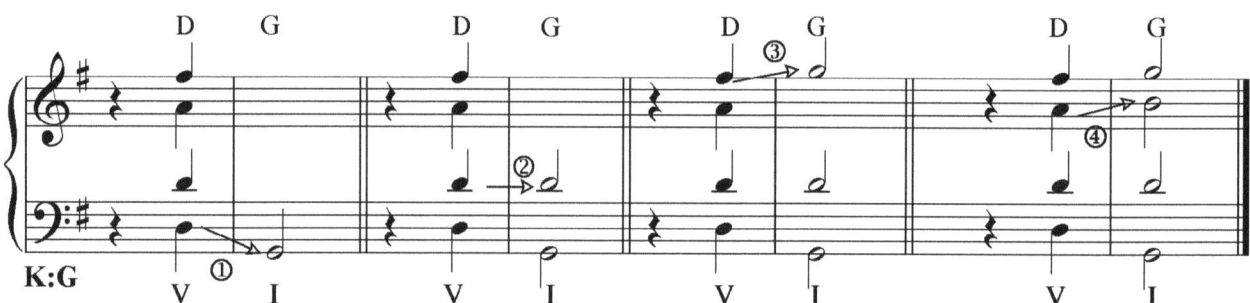

**Example Two:** In the American system this is known as an **imperfect authentic cadence** as the soprano melody finishes on a note *other than* the tonic.

# Questions on V—I Cadences (↑4) – (↓5)

### Question One
Complete these **perfect cadences (authentic cadences)** using the recipe on page 76 —
- Where possible, let the soprano part rise.
- Remember to *raise the leading note* in the **dominant chord** in a minor key.
- Indicate the moves (1- 4) between each of the parts.

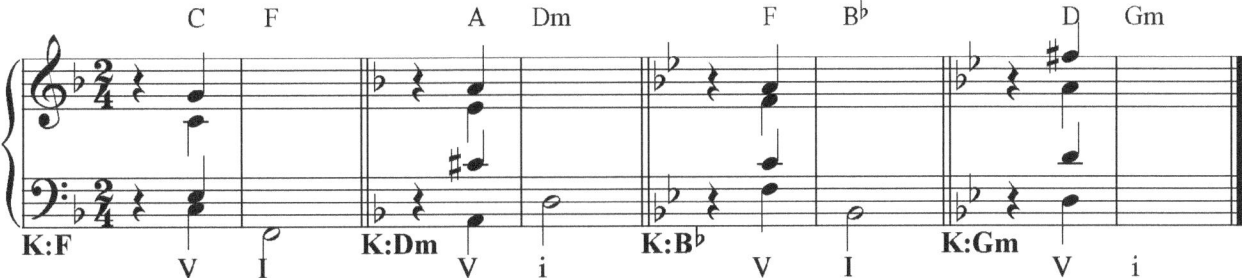

### Question Two
Write six **perfect cadences (authentic cadences)** using the recipe on page 76 —
- Write a cadence using degrees 7-8 in the soprano voice in the keys of A♭ and Fm.
- Write a cadence using degrees 2-3 in the soprano voice in the keys of B♭ and Gm.
- Write a cadence using the fifth degree as a common note in the soprano voice in the keys of A and F♯m.
- Indicate the keys and the chord names for each cadence.

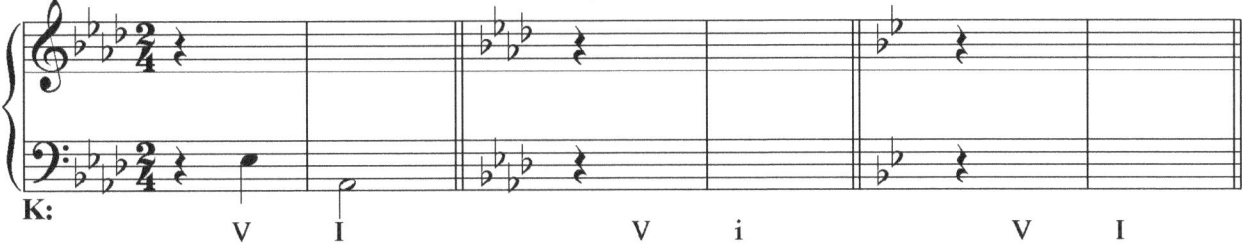

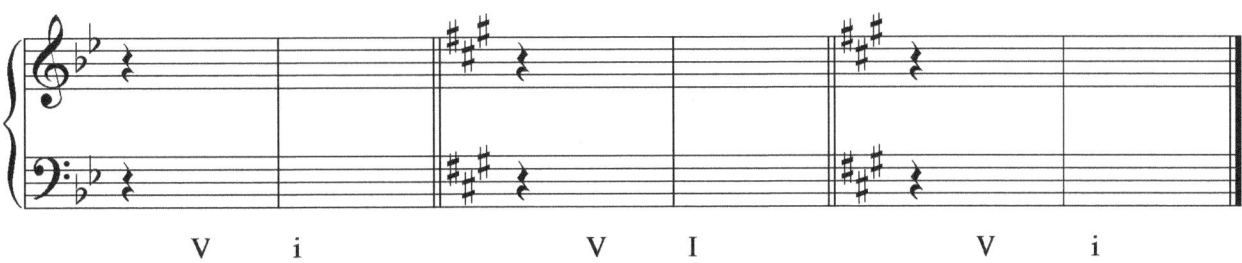

## Part Two—Resolution of a V—I Cadence Where the Melody Falls

There are two ways in which to treat the part movements
in a perfect cadence (authentic cadence) when the melody falls.

**1**
- The **first** method requires the use of the Emergency 2 voicing —
  (three root notes and one third) in the tonic chord.
- In this progression the resolution of the *leading note* (leading tone) **upwards** by step takes precedence over the use of a common note (common tone).

*Here are the recipes for writing the second chord.....*

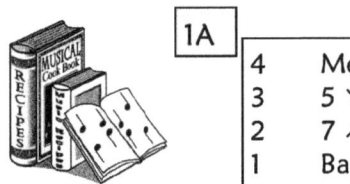

| 1A | | |
|---|---|---|
| 4 | Melody falls | 2 ↘ 1 |
| 3 | 5 ↘ 3 | |
| 2 | 7 ↗ 8 | |
| 1 | Bass Note (BN) | |

OR

| 1B | | |
|---|---|---|
| 4 | Melody falls | 5 ↘ 3 |
| 3 | 2 ↘ 1 | |
| 2 | 7 ↗ 8 | |
| 1 | BN | |

---

**2**
- In the **second** method both chords are written with the **usual voicing**.
- In this progression the *leading note* is written in an inner part and is not resolved to the tonic — it moves to the fifth degree in the tonic chord.
- This sounds OK as the leading note is *not* in the melody.
- The progression is often called a **Bach cadence** as it is frequently found in J.S Bach's harmonised chorales.

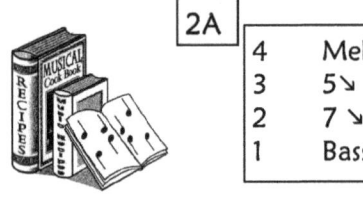

| 2A | | |
|---|---|---|
| 4 | Melody falls | 2 ↘ 1 |
| 3 | 5 ↘ 3 | |
| 2 | 7 ↘ 5 | |
| 1 | Bass Note (BN) | |

OR

| 2B | | |
|---|---|---|
| 4 | Melody falls | 5 ↘ 3 |
| 3 | 2 ↘ 1 | |
| 2 | 7 ↘ 5 | |
| 1 | Bass Note (BN) | |

**Examples - Colour-code each chord to discover the voicing.**

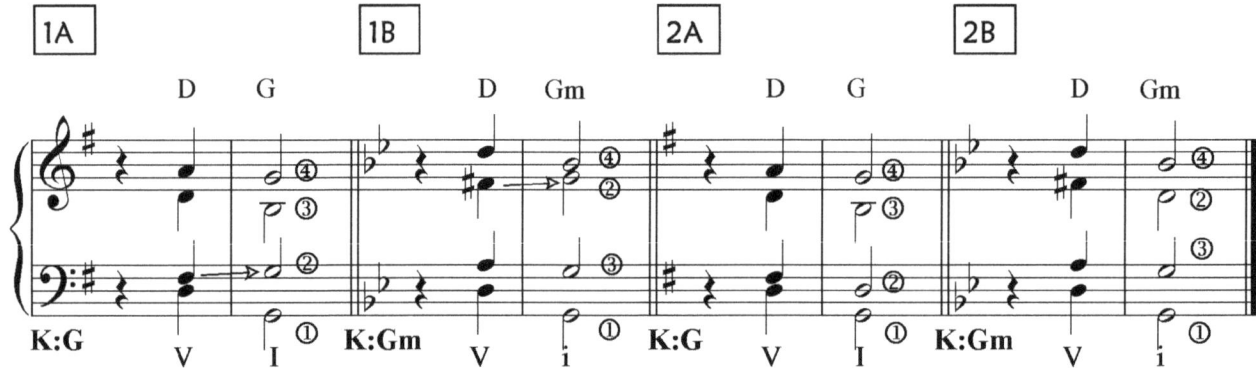

# More Questions on V—I Cadences (↑4) – (↓5)

### Question One
Complete these **perfect cadences (authentic cadences)** with falling melody lines —
- Use recipes 1A and 1B on page 78.
- Indicate the moves ( 1- 4 ) between each of the parts.

K:E♭    V   I      K:Cm    V   i      K:B    V   I      K:Fm   V   i

### Question Two
Complete these **perfect cadences (authentic cadences)** with falling melody lines —
- Use recipes 2A and 2B on page 78.
- Indicate the moves ( 1- 4 ) between each of the parts.

K:D    V   I      K:Bm   V   i      K:F    V   I      K:Dm   V   i

### Question Three - Perfect Cadences (Authentic Cadences) using chord V in first inversion
Write **V – I cadences** using the dominant chord in first inversion —
- Write the **key signature** for each bar and the **chord symbols** above each chord.
- Note that in this progression the leading note is in the bass voice and is resolved by semitone to the final tonic degree.
- The first two examples have been completed for you.
- Note the use of the *Emergency 1 voicing* (2 x 5ths) in the first example.

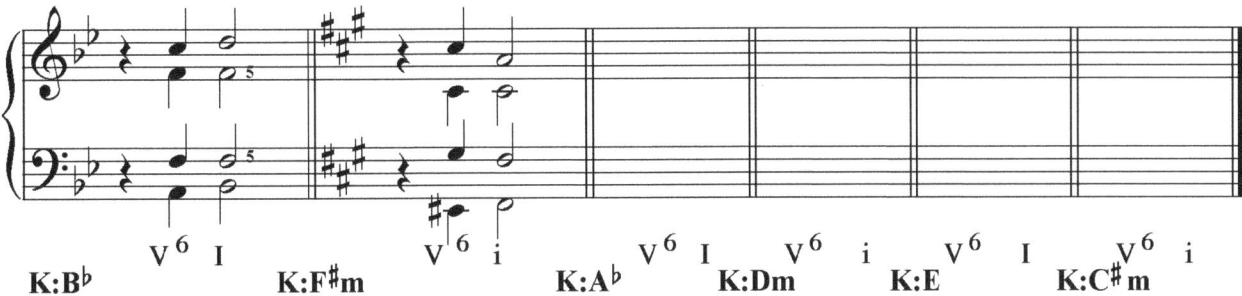

K:B♭  V⁶  I    K:F♯m  V⁶  i    K:A♭  V⁶  I    K:Dm  V⁶  i    K:E  V⁶  I    K:C♯m  V⁶  i

# Plagal Cadence

*Before commencing these exercises refer to Root Progressions—Part 3B p50*

The plagal cadence is also known as the **'amen' cadence** and is often used in church hymns.

The root movement in a **plagal cadence** is by falling fourth or rising fifth.

The plagal cadence is used as a *final* cadence, but has a less solid sound than the perfect cadence.

The root movement is *clockwise* around the Cycle of Fifths.

The movement can be tracked on the table in this manner: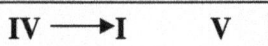

**The 'usual' resolution of a plagal cadence is shown in this diagram.**

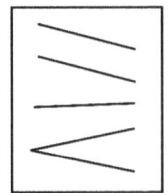

*The upper three part movements can be placed in any voice.*

This is the standard look of the progression
when both chords are in root position.

---

### 'Writing Recipe' for the Second Chord When Both Chords are in Root Position

| | |
|---|---|
| 4 | L/O ↘ |
| 3 | 4 ↘ 3 |
| 2 | CN |
| 1 | BN |

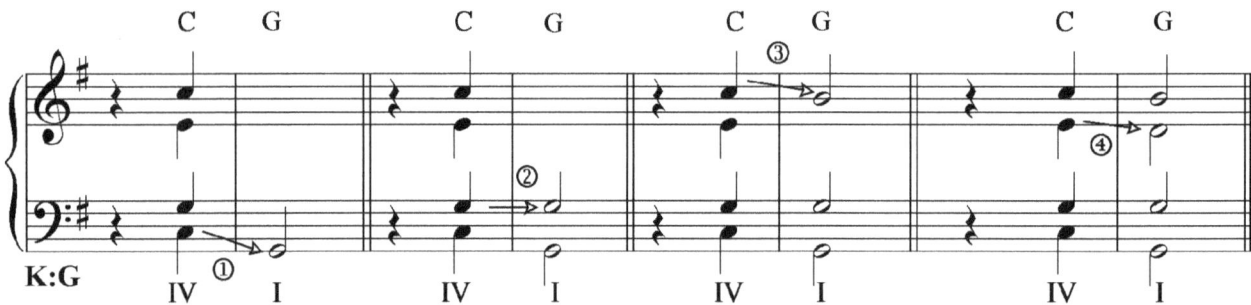

---

### Question One
- Write the remaining three voices for these **plagal cadences**.

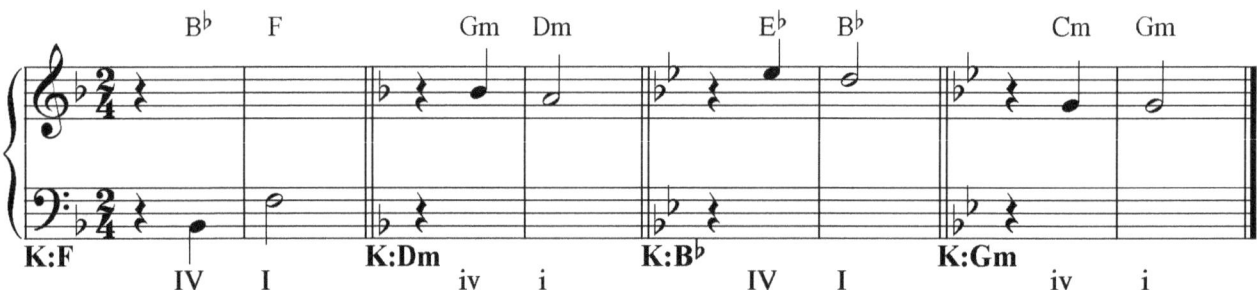

# Perfect Cadence with a Plagal Extension

Here is an example of the use of the **IV —I** progression as a **plagal extension** to a **perfect cadence (authentic cadence)**.

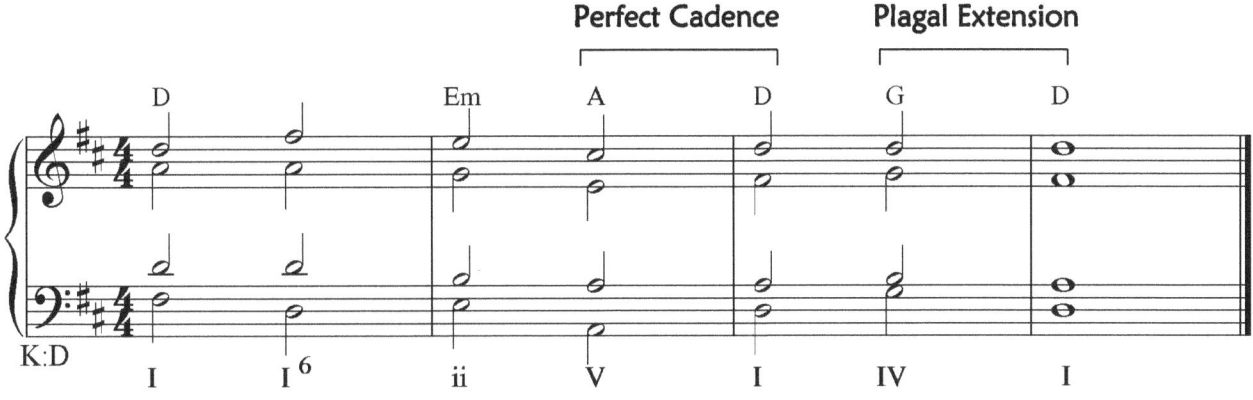

## Question Two
- First write the chord symbols.
- Next write the inner voices of these progressions.
- Put a red bracket over the chords which form the **plagal cadence**.
- Put a blue bracket over the chords which form a **perfect cadence with a plagal extension**.

## Question Three
- Identify these cadences as **perfect cadences (authentic cadences)** or **plagal cadences**.
- Include key, chord symbols and degree numbers.

Cadence: _____  _____  _____  _____

# Imperfect Cadence (Semicadence)

- There are several variations of the **imperfect cadence** (semicadence or half close).
- The common denominator is that they all finish on chord **V** of the key.
- They are used only at the end of phrases in the body of the piece.
- Another phrase is required to complete the sentence, bringing the music to rest on chord **I(i)**.
- As you have already studied their resolutions in the sections on **root movements**, they should be easy to write as they represent *only a few* of the progressions with which you are already familiar!

Notice that in the **major key chord table** all four chords that comprise the first part of the cadence are located in different vertical rows to the dominant chord.
In the **minor key chord table**, chord **ii°** (diminished) is located beneath the dominant chord.

### Major Key
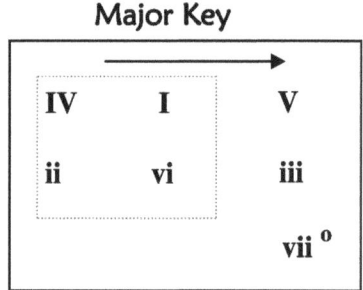

### Minor Key
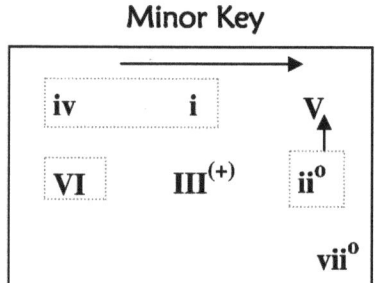

**1  Imperfect Cadence (Semicadence) — Type One**
- The first type of **imperfect cadence** is the exact reverse of the *perfect cadence.*
- The chord progression is **I (i) - V**.
- The **root progression** is the type shown in Root Progressions Part 3B, so the part movement is the same as the *plagal cadence* (rising 5th/falling 4th).

**2  Imperfect Cadence (Semicadence) — Type Two**
- The second type of **imperfect cadence** is the **ii -V** progression.
- In the minor key chord **ii** is *diminished* and therefore only used in first inversion.
- The **root progression** is the type shown in Root Progressions Part 3A. (falling 5th/rising 4th)

**3  Imperfect Cadence (Semicadence) — Type Three**
- The third type of **imperfect cadence** is the **IV (iv) -V** progression.
- The **root progression** is the type shown in Root Progressions Part 4A, (rising 2nd). It therefore requires special attention.

**4  Imperfect Cadence (Semicadence) — Type Four**
- The fourth type of **imperfect cadence** is the **vi (VI) - V** progression.
- The **root progression** is the type shown in Root Progressions Part 4B, (falling 2nd). It therefore requires special attention.
- Remember to double the *third* in chord **vi (VI)**.

## Four Types of Imperfect Cadence (Semicadence) in a Major Key

Notice the similarity between the melodic line of the soprano part in bars 1-2, 7-8 and 9-10.

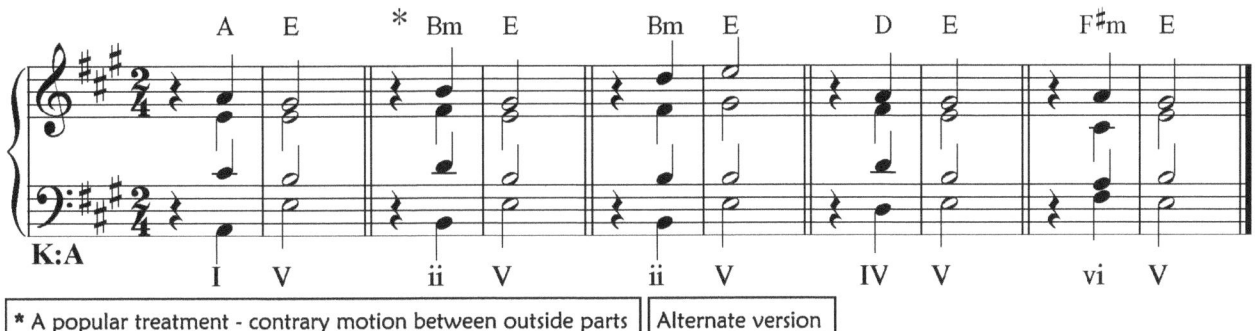

* A popular treatment - contrary motion between outside parts    Alternate version

## Four Types of Imperfect Cadence (Semicadence) in a Minor Key

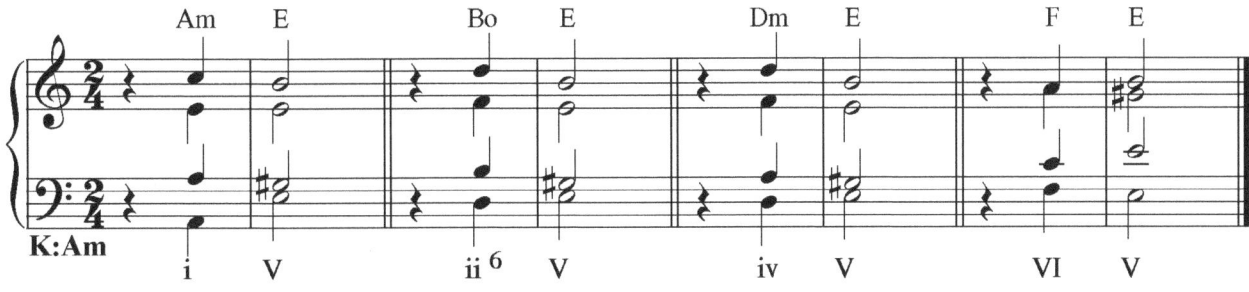

**Question One** — Write four types of **imperfect cadences** (semicadences) in a major key.

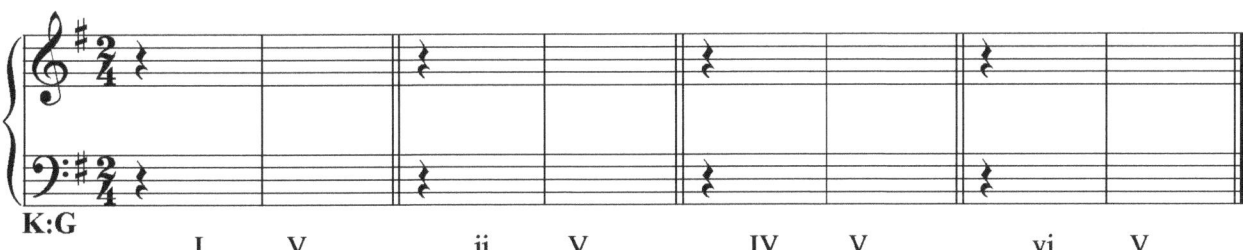

**Question Two** — Write four types of **imperfect cadences** (semicadences) in a minor key.

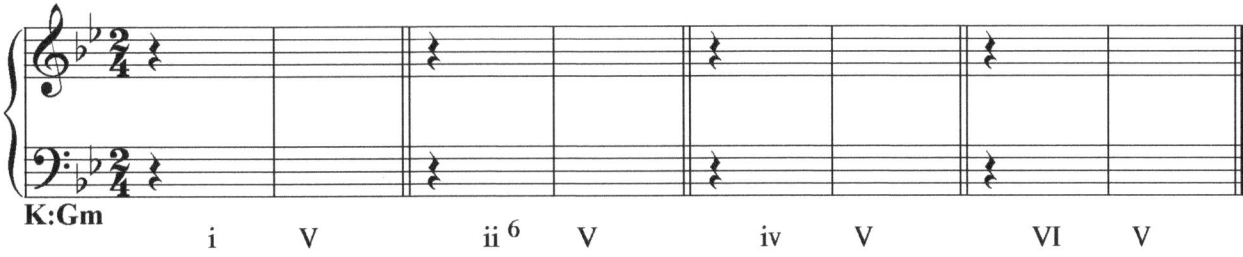

**Question Three** — Complete four different types of **imperfect cadences** to suit the soprano melody lines.

# Interrupted Cadence (Deceptive Cadence)

- The **interrupted cadence** is known by several other names including — **surprise cadence**, **abrupt cadence** and **deceptive cadence**.
- The chord movement is from **V** to **vi** (major keys) and from **V** to **VI** (minor keys).
- Review the 'writing recipe' for this progression before commencing the questions. *Refer to Root Progressions—Part 4A on page 57*.
- The chord progression *deceives* the listener into believing a **V-I(i)** cadence will follow, then *surprises* the listener when it finishes on the opposite type of chord to the tonic chord.(**vi/VI**) The music seems *interrupted* and definitely requires a balancing phrase to complete the sentence.
- It is one of the progressions which require special attention as the Root Movement is ↑2.
- Remember to **double the third degree** when chord **vi** (**VI**) appears in root position.
- The third is not necessarily doubled in chord **vi** (**VI**) when one of the chords is in an inversion.
- The progression can be tracked on the table in this manner:

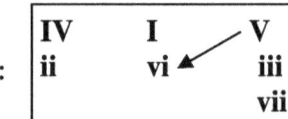

 Colour-code the doubled notes, then play and listen to these examples.
Remember when both chords are in root position, the first two writing moves are:
1) the bass note   2) 7 ↗ 8

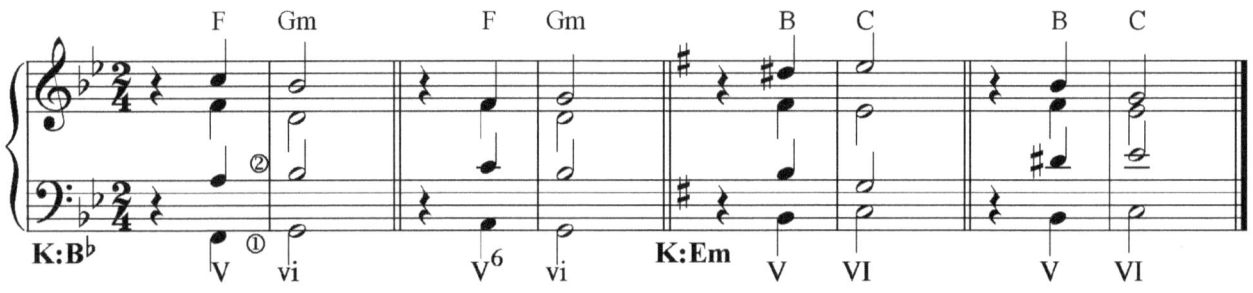

---

Question One — Complete these **interrupted (deceptive) cadences**.

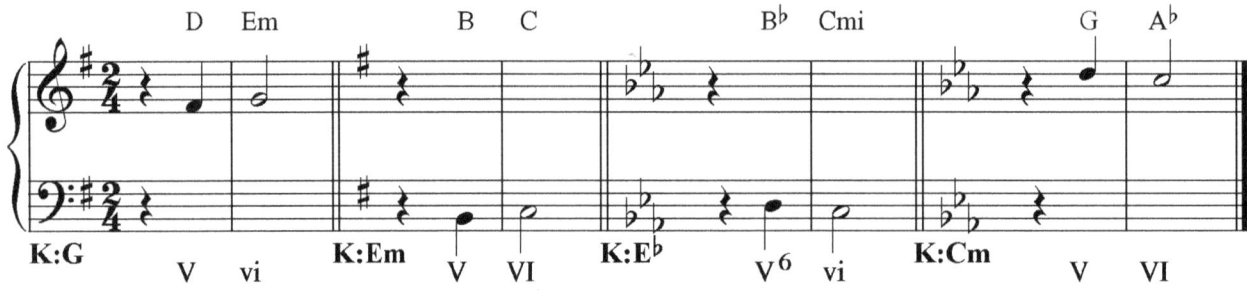

Question Two — *Cadences in Action !*

Review the musical examples in Root Progressions Part 5.
- Assess all the cadences found on pages 66 through to 69.
- Mark the cadences with a red bracket and label each one.
- Play each example to hear the effect.

# Precadential Chords

- The chord that immediately precedes the first chord in a cadence is known as a **precadential** chord (*pronounced 'pree'- cadential*).
- Chords which precede a dominant chord, are sometimes also labelled **pre-dominant chords.**
- Good choices of chord to precede chord **V**, in both the perfect and interrupted cadences, are those which appear as the first chord in an **imperfect cadence (semicadence)**.
  — *In major keys*: **I, ii IV or vi** in root position or first inversion
  — *In minor keys*: **i, iv or VI** in root position or first inversion and chord **ii⁶**
- If you choose to write chord **I(i)** as a pre-dominant chord in a **perfect** cadence, be sure to use it in *first inversion* so that the bass note is different in each of the three chords.
- To see the whole picture, refer to the examples of Intermediary cadences on page 85.
- Good choices of precadential chords before a **plagal** cadence, would be the same as above except for chord **IV(iv)**.
- The same chords could be used as precadential chords to the **imperfect cadences** (semicadences). Choose a different chord before the first cadence chord, or use two different inversions of the same chord.

## Examples of Precadential Chords

**The first chord in each of these progressions is the precadential chord.**

- Play and listen to these examples.
- Be aware of the root progressions and remember those which require 'special attention'.
- Track the chord movements on a Chord Table for the key.
- Colour-code the doubled notes.

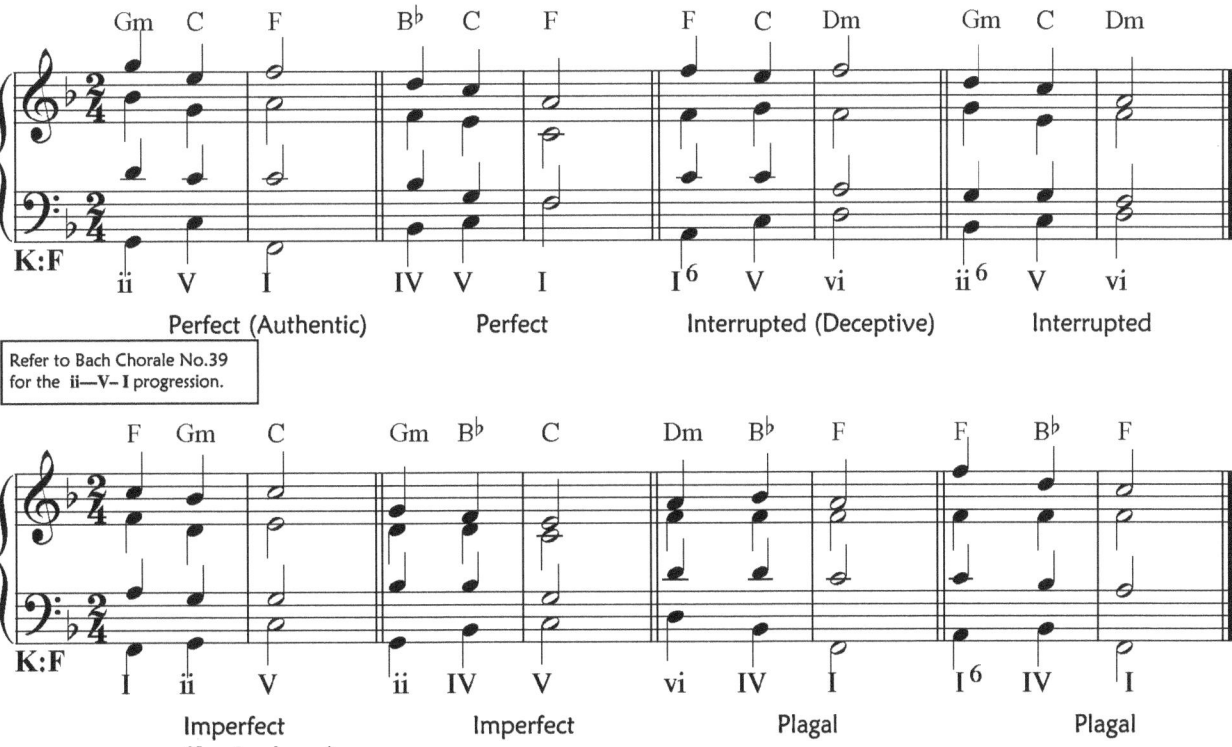

Refer to Bach Chorale No.39 for the ii—V-I progression.

# Questions on Cadences with Precadential Chords

### Question One
- Write cadences with precadential chords in the key of G minor.

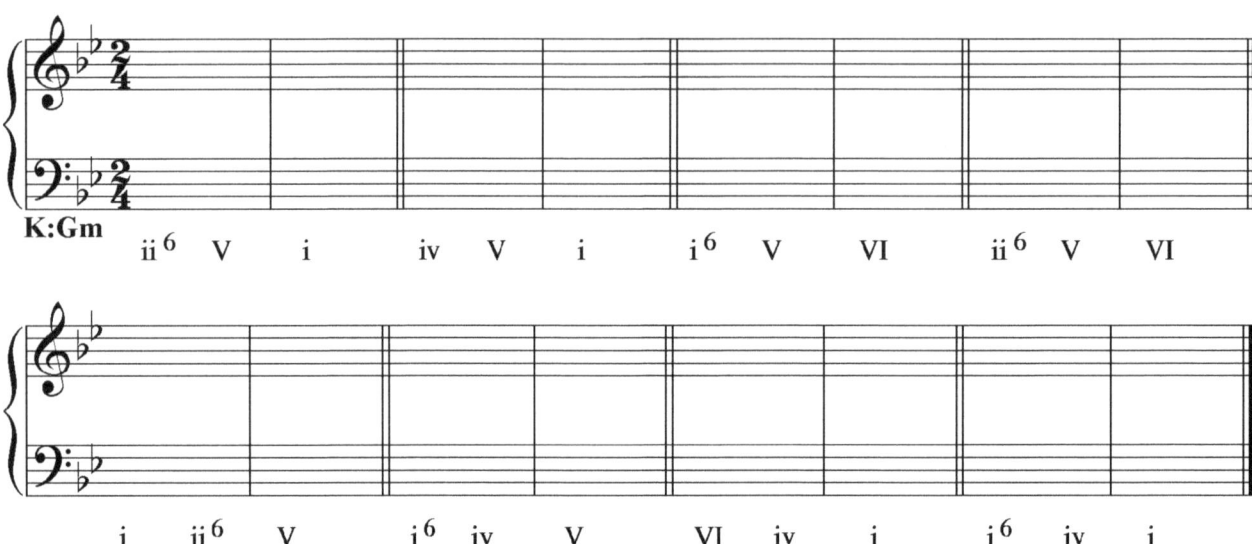

### Question Two
- Write two versions of **perfect cadences** (authentic cadences) in the keys of D Major and D minor.
- Precede each cadence with a different precadential chord.

### Question Three
- Write two versions of **interrupted cadences** in the keys of B Major and B minor.
- Precede each cadence with a different precadential chord.

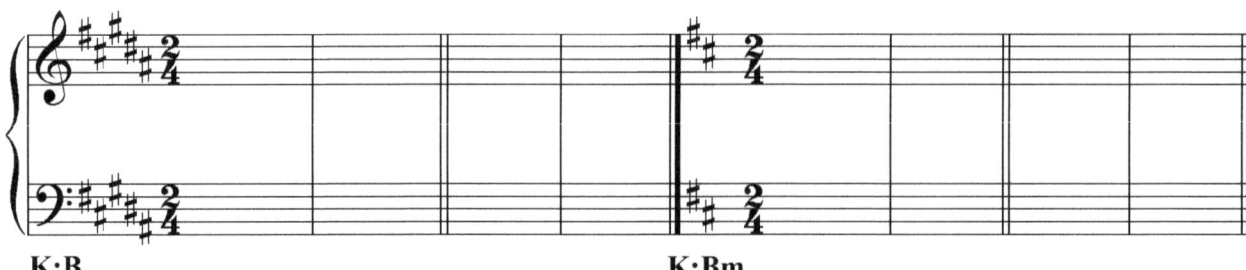

# More Cadences with Precadential Chords

### Question Four
- Write two **plagal cadences** preceded by precadential chords in the keys of A♭ Major and F minor.

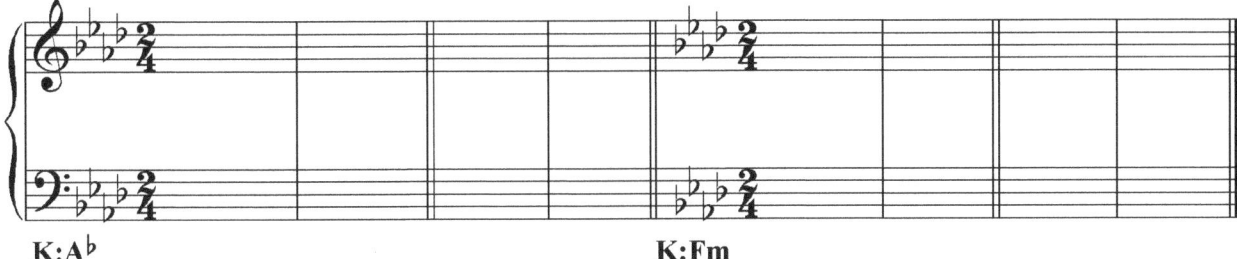

K:A♭                K:Fm

### Question Five
- Write two **imperfect cadences** (semi-cadences) in the keys of A Major and F♯ minor.
- Precede each cadence with a different precadential chord.

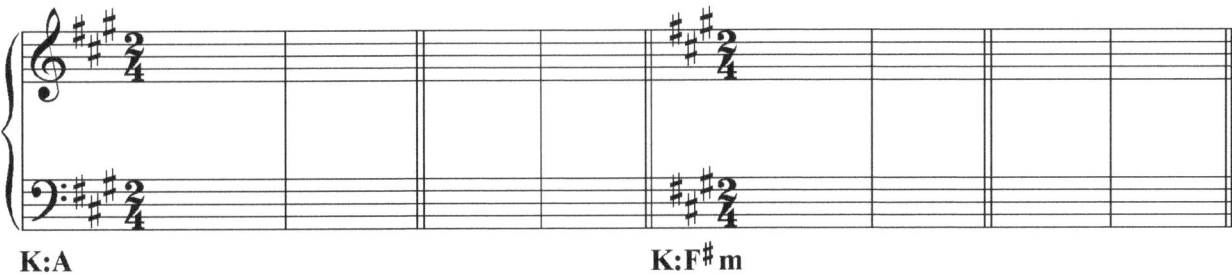

K:A                K:F♯m

### Question Six
- Write cadences to suit the given melody lines.
- Precede each cadence with a different precadential chord.
- Remember to include chord symbols, degree numbers and figuring.

K: D                K: Gm

K: Em                K: E♭

# More Cadences with Precadential Chords

**Question Seven**
- Write six cadences and precadential chords to suit the given bass lines.
- Assess each example to discover whether the progression is in a major or minor key.
- Indicate the key, chord symbols, chord degree numbers and figuring.
- The last bar in each key will require a root-position chord.
- Choose either a root-position or first-inversion chord
  for the chords in the first bar in each key.

**Question Eight**
- Write four cadences and precadential chords to suit the given bass lines.
- Assess each example to discover whether the progression is in a major or minor key.
- Supply the tonic chord for each key, written as a half note (minim).
- Indicate the key, chord symbols, chord degree numbers and figuring.

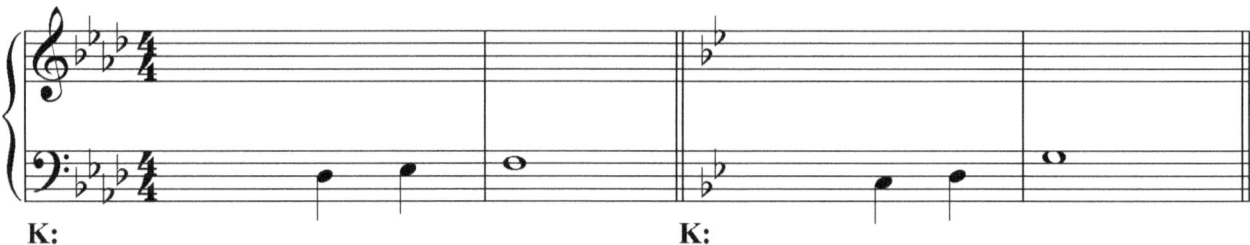

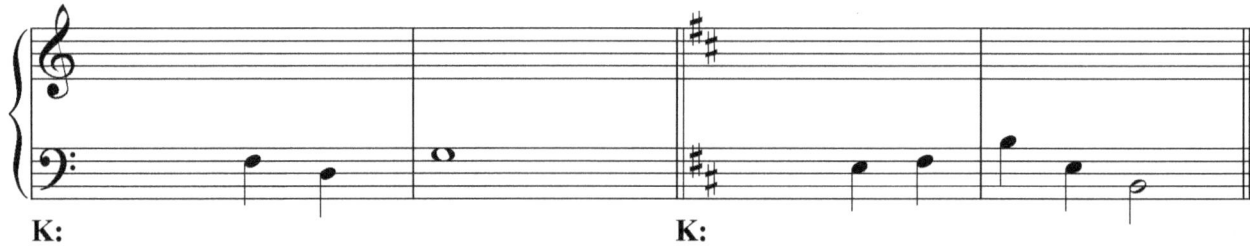

# Longer Progressions and the Basics of Two-Part Writing

 Write the upper three voices of these progressions.
- The final two bars in each of these progressions require both a cadence and a precadential chord.
- Some linking chords are required between the first chord in the progression and the arrival of the precadential chord. Be aware of the root movements and the ways learned earlier to deal with each of them.
- Write the soprano melody line first so that you can check for consecutive or exposed P5's or P8's. Aim for *contrary motion* between the outside parts wherever possible and be aware of the shape of the melody you are creating.
- At this point you will have completed a **two-part progression**. This same approach can be used if you are required to write a **melody** to a given bass line. Insert decorative notes for interest. (See both p92 and Book 2 for more techniques).

**Question One**

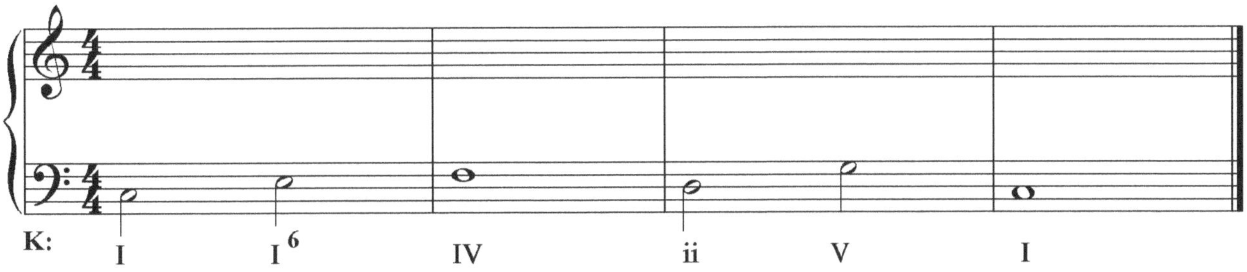

K:   I   I⁶   IV   ii   V   I

**Question Two**

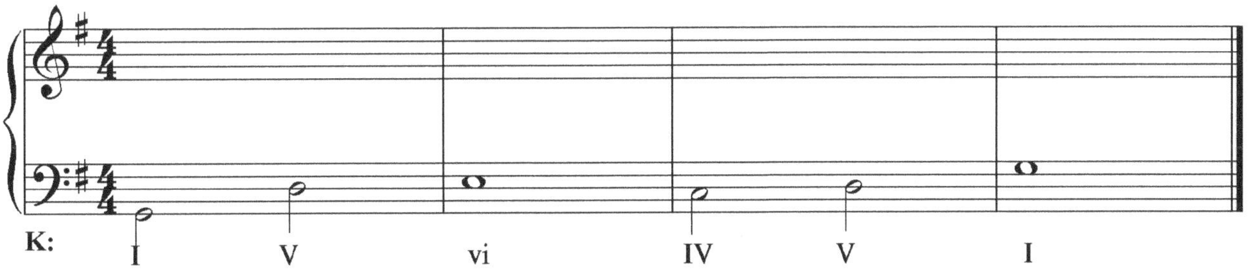

K:   I   V   vi   IV   V   I

**Question Three**

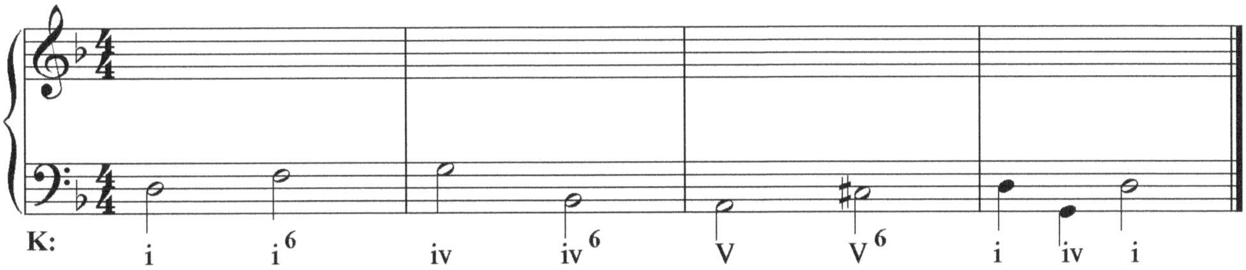

K:   i   i⁶   iv   iv⁶   V   V⁶   i   iv   i

**Question Four**

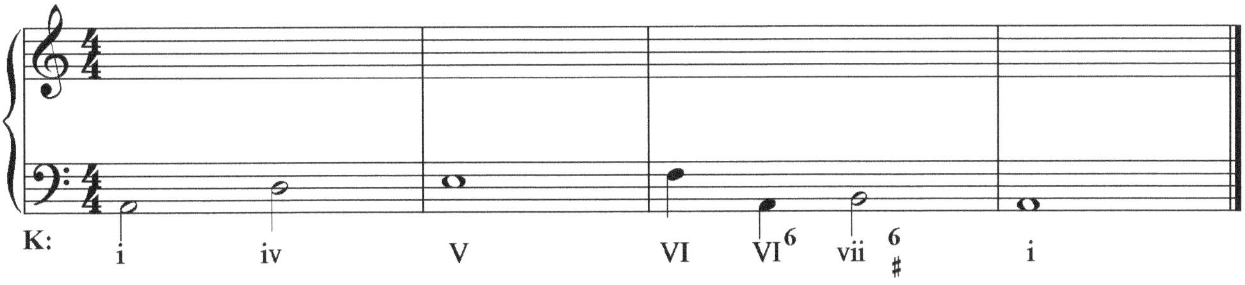

K:   i   iv   V   VI   VI⁶   vii⁶#   i

# Guidelines for the Harmonisation of a Song in Four Voices – SATB

### PREPARATION
1. Write a **chord table**
2. Indicate the **modern chord symbols** above the staff
3. Indicate the **chord degrees** below the staff

### HARMONY COMES TOGETHER — GUIDELINES

- Decide on the **first chord** for the piece and write a four-part setting of it.
- If there is an **anacrusis** your first choice of harmony would be the dominant chord provided it suits the melody note.
- The next choice could be an inversion of the tonic chord.
- Locate the **cadences** at the end of each phrase *(usually a cadence will finish on a longer note)* and choose a suitable **precadential** chord for each cadence.
- Write the **bass line** for the remainder of the piece, taking careful consideration of the chords that may apply to each melody note. Some times owing to considerations of voice leading and dangers, for instance — consecutive P5's and P8's, you may need to choose an alternative chord to the one you originally decided on.
- There may be more than one choice of chord suitable for each melody note.
- Your choice of chord may depend on where the notes are located for instance in the middle of a bar or section or at a cadence point.
- Link up the areas in between cadences using root-position and first-inversion chords.
- Check for any **'sounds to avoid'** as you do this. Refer to pages 29-35.
- Complete the task by filling in the inner voices.
- *Colour code* and then *play* the finished harmonisation to check.

## Frequently used Harmonic Devices — Voice Exchange

### Refer to Root Progressions – Part One

In the body of the piece (not at a cadence point), whenever the melody outlines a **skip or third**, which can be identified as the **first** and **third** degrees of a chord, write the bass line in *contrary motion* using the **third** and **first** degrees. This process is known as **voice-exchange**. The **root position** and **first inversion** of the same chord can be used to harmonise these degrees.

*Voice exchange is an easy-to-use harmonic device that is very neat to write.*
*The framework provides opportunities for decorative passing notes to be inserted at a later stage.*

### Examples of Voice Exchange with Passing Notes Inserted

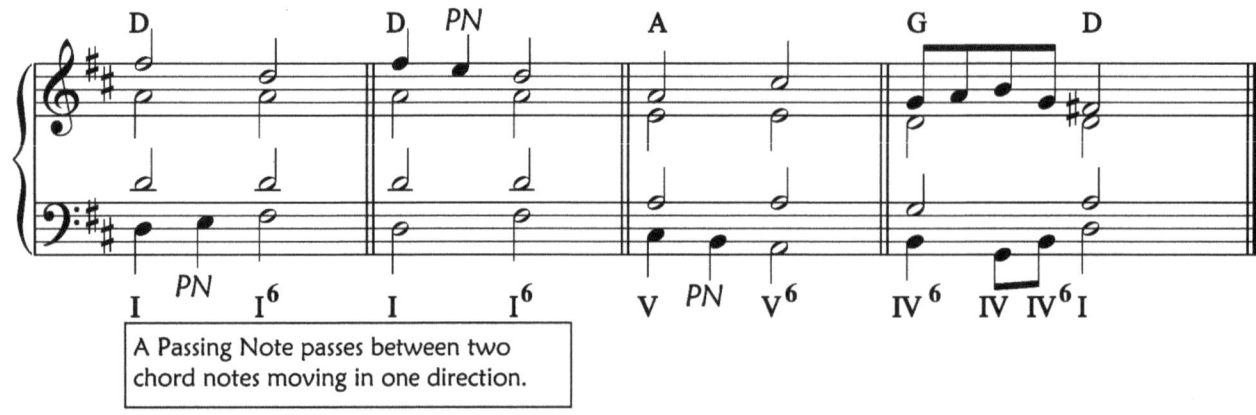

A Passing Note passes between two chord notes moving in one direction.

# Harmonisation of the Melody – *Portsmouth*

 Follow the procedure outlined on the previous page to complete the harmonisation.

- The bass line has been done for you.
- In this tune, the end of the first phrase is in bar four and is indicated with a *caesura* (which looks like a comma).
- **Colour code** and **play** the finished harmonisation to check.
- A completed version of the harmonisation appears on page 96. This is one of the ways in which the tune may be harmonized.
- Compare *your* version with the one on page 96.

---

**Harmony Comes Together — STICKY SITUATION — RESCUE CARD**

— **Consecutive P5's** can sometimes be corrected by **inverting** them so they become consecutive P4's. Place the notes in different voices to achieve this.

— A **bye-tone** (another note of the chord) can be inserted to avoid a consecutive P5 or P8.

— **Overlapping is permitted** between two settings of the same chord.

 - This is useful when the melody includes a large leap, as in bar two.
 *(Bar One is the first full bar after the anacrusis.)*

---

## PORTSMOUTH
### Traditional English Folk Tune

K:G

# Harmonisation of the melody — *Flow Gently, Sweet Afton*

To complete the harmonisation of this melody, follow the guidelines on page 92.
- Compare your version to the completed harmonisation on page 97.
- There may be other correct answers.

**Harmonisation Tip**
- *Bars 1, 2 & 3* may each be harmonised with a single chord in different positions.

## FLOW GENTLY, SWEET AFTON
Traditional Scottish Folk Song

# Harmonisation of the melody —
## *Grün, Grün, Grün Sind Alle Meine Kleider*
## *(All my clothes are green, green, green.)*

- To complete the harmonisation of this melody, follow the guidelines on page 92.
- Compare your version to the completed harmonisation on page 98.

> **Harmonisation Tip**
> *Look for opportunities to use the **ii V I** progression.*

### GRÜN, GRÜN, GRÜN SIND ALLE MEINE KLEIDER
Traditional German Folk Song

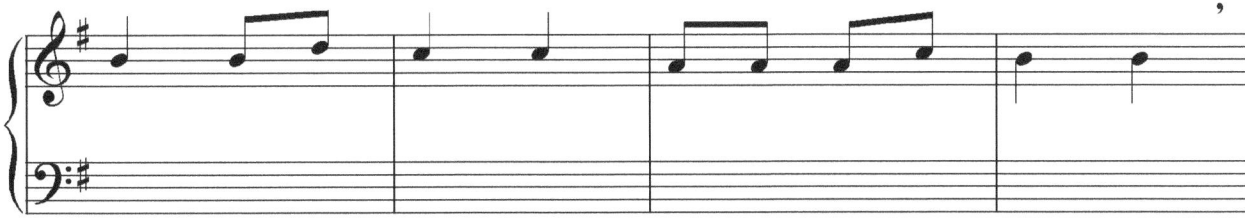

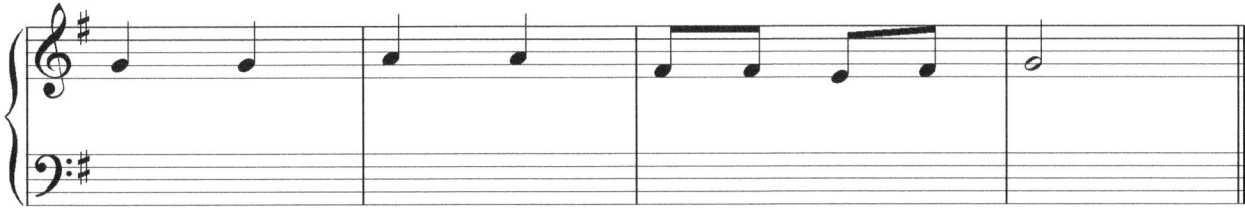

# Answer Page 1

 Harmony in Action!  Page 26 - Completed exercise

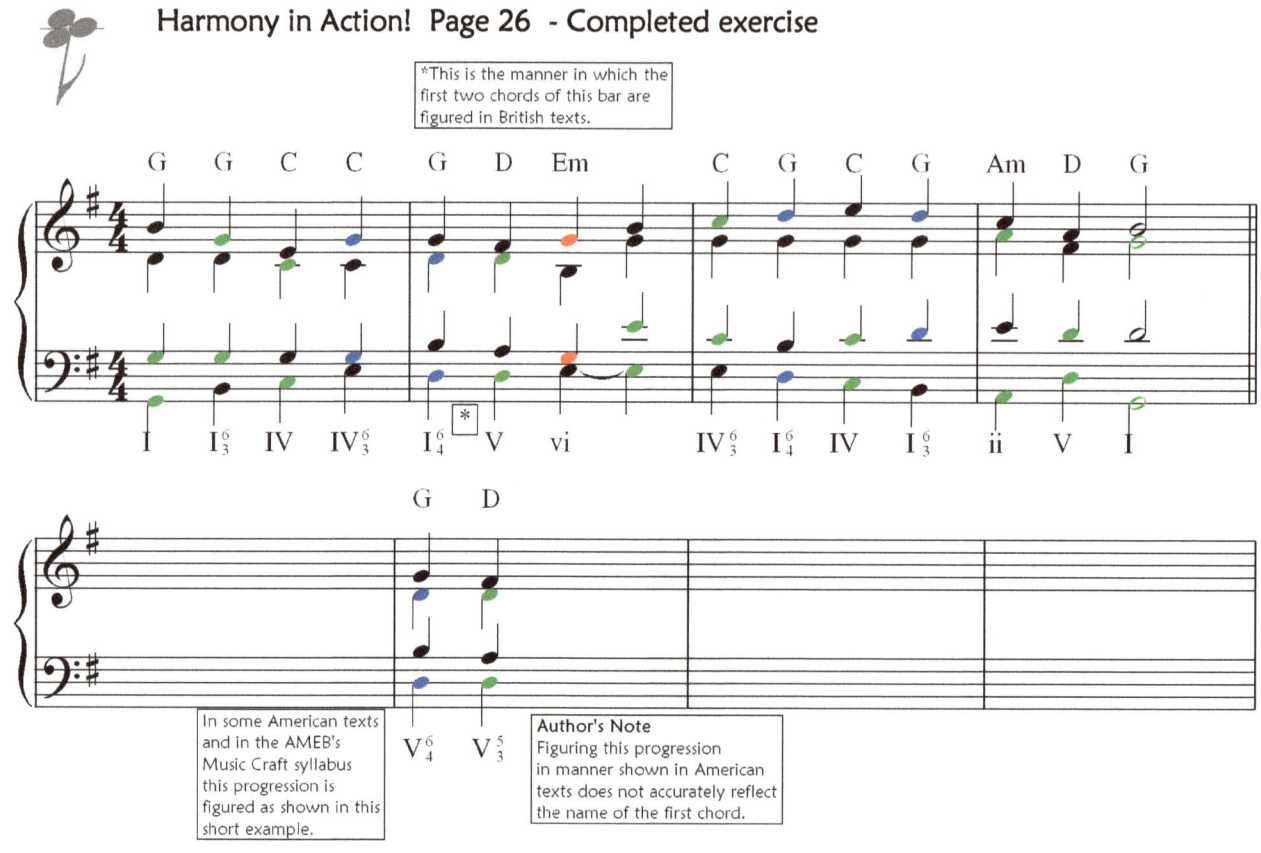

Here is a completed harmonisation of *Portsmouth* which appears on page 93.

- Some passing notes have been inserted for interest.
- Note the use of different positions of the same harmony.
- *Colour-code the setting to discover the voicings.*

### PORTSMOUTH

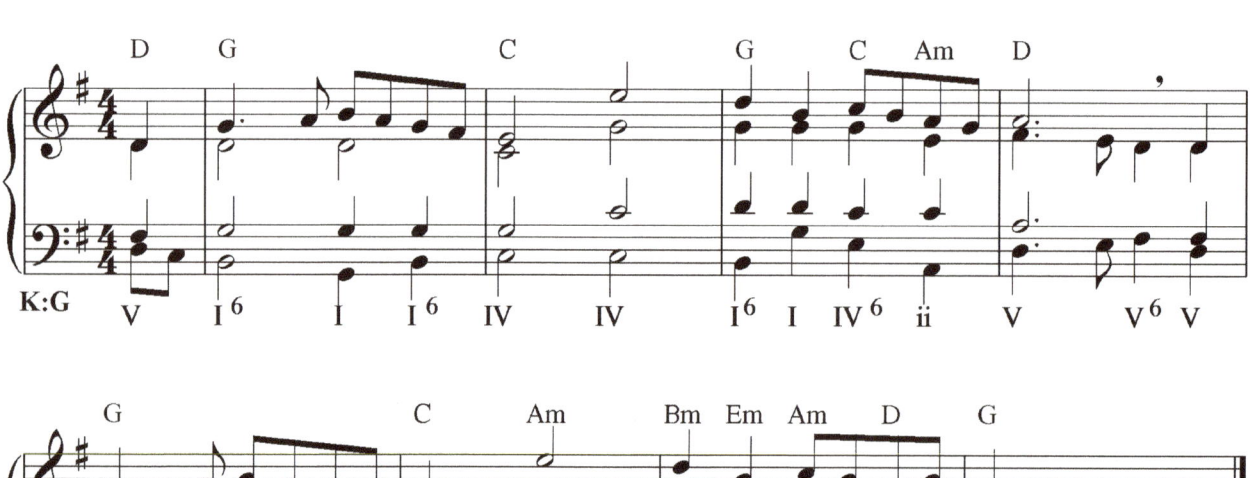

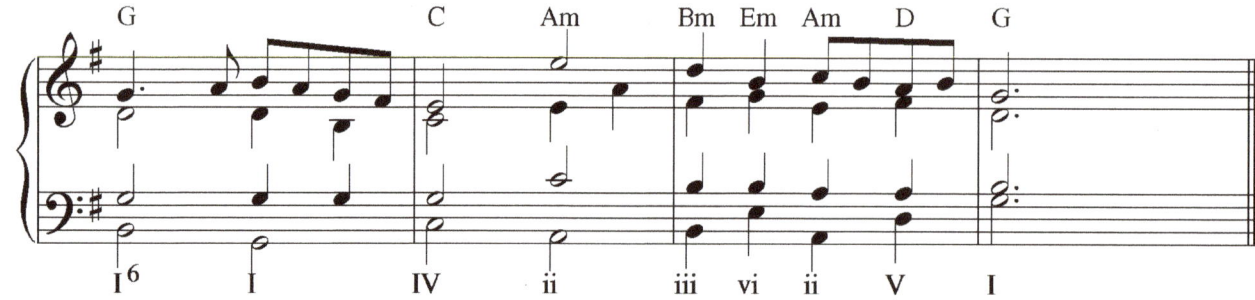

# Answer Page 2

Here is a completed harmonisation of *Flow Gently, Sweet Afton* from page 94.

- Some passing notes have been inserted for interest—see bars 1, 9, 10 and 11.
- Note the use of different positions of the same harmony.
- *Colour-code the setting to discover the voicings.*

## FLOW GENTLY, SWEET AFTON

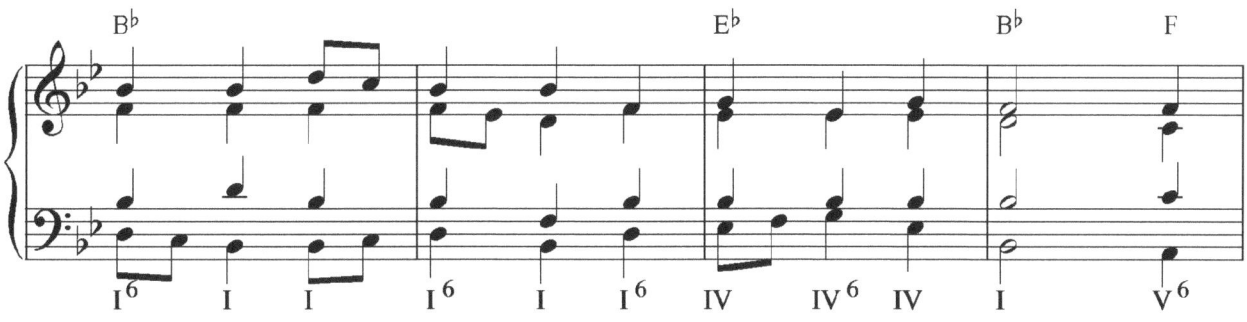

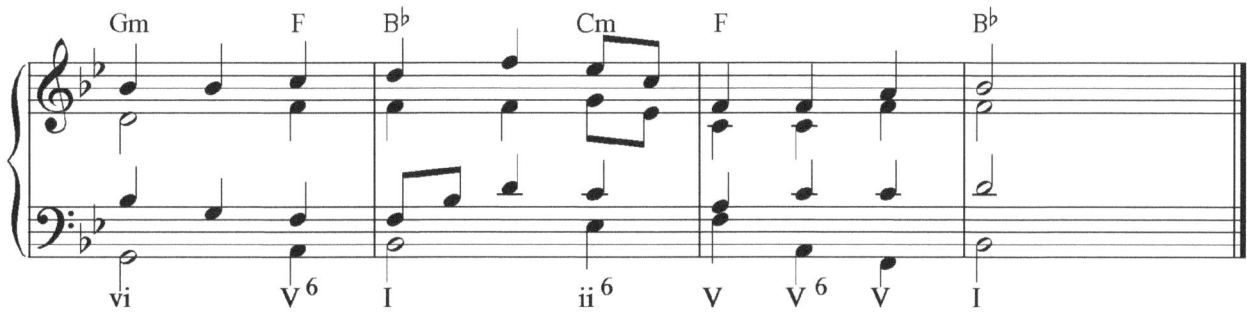

# Answer Page 3

**Here is a completed harmonisation of *Grün, Grün, Grün Sind Alle Meine Kleider* on p98.**
- Some passing notes have been inserted for interest.
- Note the *ascending* stepwise Root Progression in bars 9-12.
- Also note the use of the **ii V I** section of the **cycle progression** in several places.
- *Colour-code the setting to discover the voicings.*

### GRÜN, GRÜN, GRÜN SIND ALLE MEINE KLEIDER

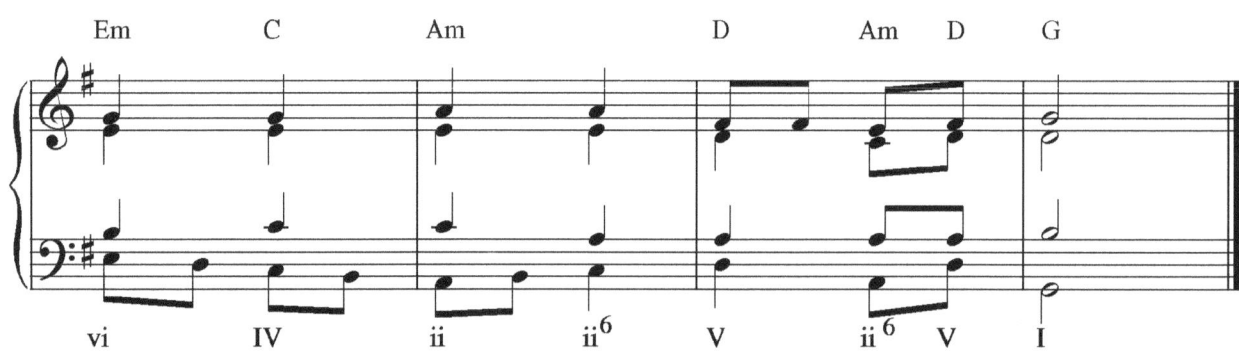

# HARMONY COMES TOGETHER

## PREVIEW OF BOOK TWO

Congratulations on completing *Harmony Comes Together—Book One*

You are now ready to commence Book Two of this series.

Topics in Book Two include:

1) **Decorative notes** — passing notes, auxiliary notes (neighbour tones)

2) **Practical harmonic analysis**

3) **Progressions using second inversion chords** $^6_4$

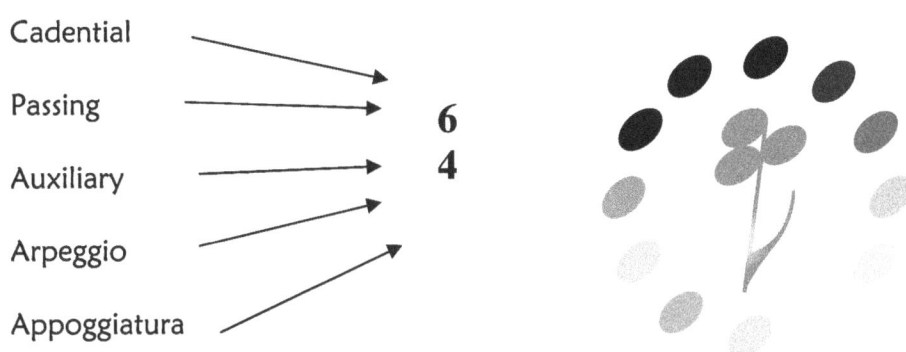

Cadential
Passing
Auxiliary
Arpeggio
Appoggiatura

$\rightarrow$ $^6_4$

4) **Scale-tone seventh chords:**

 — Dominant 7th chord and its use in progressions
 — Inversions of the Dominant 7th
 — Resolving the Dominant 7th around the Cycle of Fifths

 Secondary 7th and Added 6th chords:
 Major Seventh, Minor Seventh & Diminished Seventh
 Half-diminished Seventh, Major Sixth and Minor Sixth

5) **Dominant extension chords**

6) **Dominant substitution chords**

7) **Melodic decoration**

8) **Suspensions**

9) **Modulation**

# Harmony Comes Together – Extra Practice Page

www.ingramcontent.com/pod-product-compliance
Lightning Source LLC
Chambersburg PA
CBHW041131240426
43661CB00068B/2911